MAIN LINES & BRANCHES

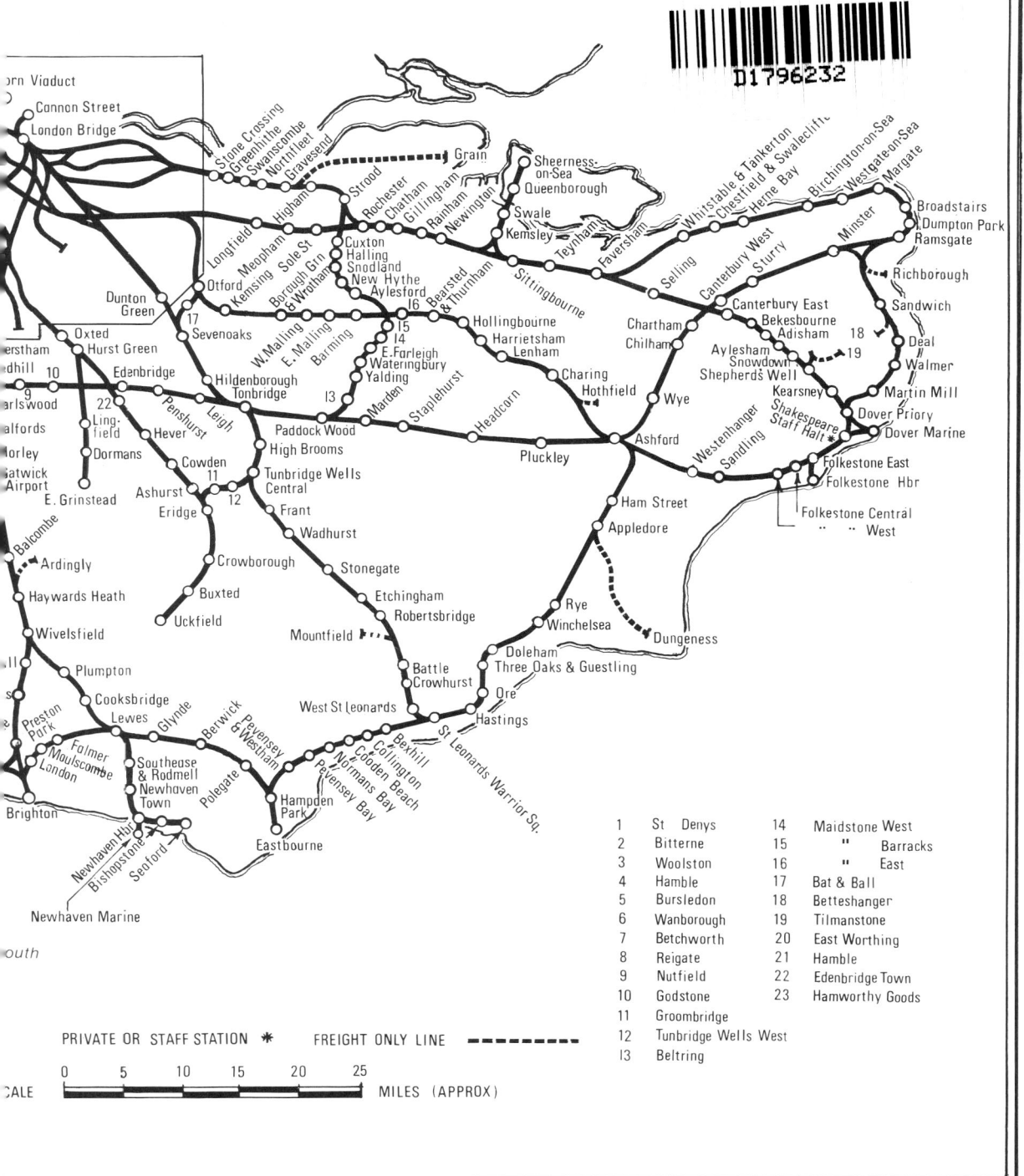

D1796232

1	St Denys	14	Maidstone West
2	Bitterne	15	" Barracks
3	Woolston	16	" East
4	Hamble	17	Bat & Ball
5	Bursledon	18	Betteshanger
6	Wanborough	19	Tilmanstone
7	Betchworth	20	East Worthing
8	Reigate	21	Hamble
9	Nutfield	22	Edenbridge Town
10	Godstone	23	Hamworthy Goods
11	Groombridge		
12	Tunbridge Wells West		
13	Beltring		

PRIVATE OR STAFF STATION ✳ FREIGHT ONLY LINE – – – – – – –

SCALE 0 5 10 15 20 25 MILES (APPROX)

Southern
RAILS IN THE 1980s

Southern
RAILS IN THE 1980s

Colin J. Marsden

LONDON
IAN ALLAN LTD

Contents

Introduction	4
Main Lines	5
Inter Regional Workings	43
Commuter Services	48
Branch Lines	66
Cross-Country Workings	72
Freight Traffic	80
Locomotive & Stock Maintenance	92
Behind the Scenes	100

First published 1983

ISBN 0 7110 1331 4

All rights reserved. No part of this book may be reproduced or transmitted in any form or by any means, electronic or mechanical, including photo-copying, recording or by any information storage and retrieval system, without permission from the Publisher in writing.

© Ian Allan Ltd 1983

Published by Ian Allan Ltd, Shepperton, Surrey; and printed by Ian Allan Printing Ltd at their works at Coombelands in Runnymede, England

Introduction

This is the second book in the 'Rails in the 1980s' series reviewing the Southern Region scene. The boundaries of coverage are those routes or sections owned by the SR, and although some changes have taken place during the 1980s all areas under the control of the SR Board from 1 January 1980 have been included.

The book has been divided into various sections taking the reader for a train ride throughout the system, firstly on the main lines and then on the inter-regional workings, commuter services, branch lines and cross-country routes. The last three sections have been devoted to the operations of a modern railway that the public may not be aware of, including freight traffic, locomotive and stock maintenance and behind the scenes covering various development, trials and departmental operations. Each chapter of the book has its own introduction.

I would like to express my gratitude to the following people who have assisted me with the preparation of this volume: Mr John Faulkner MCIT, for supplying the majority of the section introductory material, to the SR Press Office at Waterloo for furnishing some of the facts and figures of the region, to various photographers who have sent material for inclusion, and to the publishers for giving me freedom of selection of material for this book. I hope that followers of the SR will find this publication of interest and enjoy reading it as much as I have enjoyed preparing it.

Colin J. Marsden
Surbiton
January 1983

Main Lines

The latest pocket diagram designates six Inter-City routes on the Southern Region: Waterloo-Salisbury-Exeter, Waterloo-Bournemouth-Weymouth, Waterloo-Portsmouth, Victoria-Brighton, Victoria-Chatham-Dover, Charing Cross-Ashford-Dover and Canterbury. Whether included as Inter-City or not, all the Southern Region's main lines are also involved in the daily movement of commuters into and out of London and the regular service pattern has then to be subordinated to their requirements.

The longest and most important Inter-City route within the SR is the South Western Division's line from Waterloo to Bournemouth and Weymouth, electrified over the 108 miles to Bournemouth in 1967. It now carries an hourly express service covering the 79 miles to Southampton in 67 minutes and reaching Bournemouth in 96 minutes. Here the Class 430 (4REP) unit which has propelled the train from Waterloo is detached and a Class 33/1 diesel locomotive couples on in front to the one or two Class 491 (4TC) sets which continue over the non-electrified line to Weymouth, calling at all stations. Ten minutes behind the express a semi-fast train leaves Waterloo serving principal stations to Bournemouth, including Southampton Airport for flights to the Channel Islands.

The REP/TC stock is based on BR Mk I vehicles and plans are in hand to replace it with Mk III type stock during the mid-1980's. Schedules were slightly accelerated in 1979 and as much of the well-engineered London and Southampton main line is suitable for 100mph running, it should be possible with modern rolling stock and good track maintenance to cut these times still further. The service is completed by half-hourly stopping trains, formed usually of Class 423 (4VEP) stock, which run fast to Woking stopping at Surbiton. At Woking an Alton portion is detached, the stopping Bournemouth train then calls at all stations to

Basingstoke where one service per hour terminates while the other continues to Bournemouth, pausing at Southampton to let the fast service overtake.

Portsmouth is only 74 miles from Waterloo but has never enjoyed such good train services as its neighbour, Southampton. The best timing that is currently operated over the scenic and switchback Portsmouth Direct line is 86 minutes between Waterloo and Portsmouth & Southsea by the hourly semi-fast train calling at Woking, Guildford, Haslemere and Havant. During the 1970s a second hourly train with fewer stops was provided but failed to attract sufficient patronage and there seems to be little scope for further reduction of running times due to the severe gradients and speed restrictions of the route. The usual stock for the semi-fast service is a 12-car formation of Class 421 and 420 (4CIG/BIG/CIG) units. Half-hourly departures from Waterloo are maintained by a train running fast to Woking and Guildford then calling at most intermediate stations to Portsmouth, formed of either Class 421 or 423 stock. Stations between Guildford and Portsmouth are also served by an extension of one of the half-hourly Waterloo-Guildford stopping trains, which connects with the semi-fast from Waterloo. Some of these Waterloo-Portsmouth stopping trains take the Cobham route to Guildford during the peak period. Sunday services on the Bournemouth and Portsmouth lines have been the subject of recent economy cuts, especially during the winter, with Bournemouth fast trains limited to evening workings and many stations on the Portsmouth line closed until mid-afternoon.

The Waterloo-Salisbury-Exeter service provides the only regular appearance of diesel traction at Waterloo. The Exeter trains are formed of WR based Mk II air braked stock and since May 1981 have been powered by WR Class 50 locomotives from Laira depot. Semi-fast between Waterloo and

Salisbury, the two-hourly trains then call at almost every surviving station on the single line to Exeter. The use of the Class 50s has enabled schedules to be cut by about 20 minutes to give a best time to Exeter Central of 196 minutes for the 172 miles, including 11 intermediate stops. When a 2,700hp '50' is not available haulage usually reverts to the previous motive power, a SR Class 33 of 1,550hp, so that a loss of time is inevitable.

During 1981/2 the service between Waterloo and Salisbury was increased to an hourly frequency by the addition of trains calling at Woking, Basingstoke and all stations beyond. These trains have a variety of formations; one of the WR Exeter sets with a Class 50 which berths overnight at Salisbury, the stock of the 01.40 Waterloo-Yeovil newspaper train making additional daytime runs to and from Salisbury hauled by a Class 33 locomotive, and push-pull trains formed of a Class 491 (TC) set and a Class 33/1 diesel. Two of these push-pull trains have Monday to Friday peak hour departures from Waterloo combined with EMUs bound for Eastleigh and Bournemouth which are detached at Basingstoke while the diesel locomotive and the TC set at the head of the train proceed to Salisbury.

The improvement to the Salisbury service strengthens the case for electrification of the $33\frac{1}{2}$ miles from Worting Junction. This would eliminate diesel traction at Waterloo and by adopting the REP/TC method, the unpowered vehicles could go forward from Salisbury behind WR diesel locomotives with minimum delay.

The once numerous Ocean Liner Expresses to Southampton Docks have dwindled to occasional trains in connection with the summer transatlantic crossings of the *QE2* and the sailings of the *Canberra* and other cruise liners. A small pool of hauled stock is based at Clapham Junction for these, including one train of early Mk II first class coaches. Specials to the docks are worked by either Class 33 diesels or Class 73 electro-diesels, which use their diesel engines within the dock boundaries.

A seasonal boat train runs between Waterloo and Weymouth Quay in connection with the Channel Islands sailings. This usually has Class 73 haulage as far as Bournemouth and a Class 33/1 thence, including the much-photographed passage through the streets of Weymouth to the Quay. During the winter months a bus link is provided between the Town station and the Quay. For London traffic the

Weymouth route is being overtaken by the new service from Portsmouth, where rail connections are provided by the ordinary semi-fast trains from Waterloo to Portsmouth Harbour with a bus to the ferry terminal.

Central Division services were radically reorganised in 1978 but this new timetable has seldom operated as planned. The Victoria resignalling, the track alterations in the Croydon area associated with the Three Bridges signalling scheme, and the engineering works at Victoria in connection with the new air terminal have caused successive alterations to the timetable with frequent delays, curtailments and diversions, notably of Victoria services to London Bridge over an extended period.

The 1978 timetable was based on the major traffic centres of East Croydon and Gatwick Airport which have developed since the pattern of electric services was first established in the 1930s. In the basic Monday to Friday service all trains now call at East Croydon and, except for the hourly fast to Brighton, all now stop at Gatwick Airport to provide connections to the South Coast. From Victoria, Gatwick is served four times per hour (also hourly throughout the night) by Gatwick portions formed of Class 427 (4VEG) sets, adapted to provide additional luggage space. These portions are detached at Gatwick from semi-fast trains bound for Brighton, Horsham or Bognor.

When the new Air Terminal at Victora is completed in 1984 push-pull trains formed of Mk II stock with Class 73 electro-diesels will shuttle between its two distinct platforms and Gatwick Airport. No more problems of matching airport portions to late running coastal services and no more conflict between air travellers and commuters.

The standard off-peak pattern of service provides four trains per hour between London and Brighton; a fast, a semi-fast (temporarily diverted to London Bridge), and two trains serving all stations beyond Gatwick. Half-hourly stopping trains from London Bridge via Tulse Hill terminate at Redhill, leaving Redhill to Gatwick with a local service in peak hours only.

The other radial routes to Eastbourne and Hastings, to Worthing and Littlehampton and to Bognor and Portsmouth, all have hourly semi-fast services. All off-peak Mid Sussex line trains now run via Gatwick, the Dorking route is only served by

Monday to Friday commuter trains and by Saturday services diverted from the East Croydon area. During the present engineering works the weekend services differ considerably from the mid-week pattern. Besides acting as a diversion for Victoria, London Bridge still plays its traditional part as the terminus for City-bound commuters, but normally sees little main line activity outside peak hours.

The standard stock for the fast services are the Class 420/421 units, supplemented by a few Class 410 (4BEP) buffet car sets; refreshment facilities on the Central Division are still quite numerous on Mondays to Fridays. Slower trains should be formed of Class 423 stock but the Class 427 units often stray from their assigned Victoria-Gatwick run. When the original PAN/PUL stock was replaced in the mid-1960s the traditional 60 minute non-stop timing to Brighton was reduced to 55 minutes. With the inclusion of an East Croydon stop and the addition of some recovery time for engineering works the current best is 58 minutes. When the new signalling is ready and the track layout has been rationalised between Croydon and Coulsdon, some progress should be possible towards the mile-a-minute journey to Brighton.

Despite threats of closure, the Newhaven to Dieppe cross-channel service still provides an alternative route between London and Paris. Throughout most of the year a special boat train, now composed of EMU stock, departs from the South Eastern side of Victoria returning there in the evening via the Stewarts Lane low level lines.

The South Eastern Division main line services are still largely based on the routes operated by the SER and LCDR prior to the merger of 1899. From Charing Cross down the SER main line (electrified in 1961) there is an hourly fast train calling at Waterloo, Ashford, Folkestone Central and terminating at Dover Priory. The 70 miles to Folkestone are covered in 77 minutes, three minutes less than the SECR 'L' class 4-4-0s were achieving 60 years ago without the Ashford stop. A semi-fast departure from Charing Cross 30 minutes later continues round the coast from Dover to Ramsgate and also detaches at Ashford a portion for Ramsgate via Canterbury West. Surprisingly the promotion of the Ashford-Canterbury route to Inter-City status in 1982 coincided with the transfer of its through services from the fast to the semi-fast trains from Charing Cross. The main line service is completed

by an hourly train for Ashford calling at all stations beyond Sevenoaks.

The Tonbridge-Hastings line failed to meet Southern Railway criteria for electrification in 1937 and replacement of steam traction had to await the introduction in 1957 of 23 narrow profile diesel-electric multiple-units. These are now nearing the end of their working lives and their replacement poses an acute problem. The choice is between (1) to build more non-standard narrow diesel stock designed to fit the tunnels, (2) to single the restrictive tunnels so as to accommodate either normal diesel units eg: Class 210, or standard SR EMU stock after electrification, (3) to close the line beyond Tunbridge Wells. Although the off-peak frequency was reduced in the 1981/82 service from half-hourly to hourly the peak hour traffic through Tunbridge Wells makes single line operation impracticable here and BR have sought powers to bore a duplicate tunnel. Whether finance will be forthcoming for this or for electrification is another question. In the event of closure Hastings would be served by the trains from Victoria via Eastbourne, taking 13-30 minutes longer.

On the Chatham route the 1982 summer timetable brought the first major restructuring of fast services since electrification in 1959. Instead of combined trains for Thanet and Dover splitting at Faversham, a half-hourly service from Victoria runs alternately to each line making a cross-platform interchange there with a stopping train for the other route. The Victoria-Dover trains run through to Dover Western Docks (formerly Marine) to provide a rail link to the port for travellers not using the special boat trains. As with most SR electrification projects, the result was increased frequency of service but little reduction in overall journey times. On the Chatham line commuter traffic has grown at intermediate stations such as Rainham and Sittingbourne; even without additional stops the LCDR track was never laid out for high speed.

The other LCDR route via Maidstone East has two trains an hour from Victoria, one fast to Maidstone then all stations to Ashford, Canterbury and Ramsgate, and the other slow to Maidstone only. Trains on this line are now independent of services on the Chatham route and the Region was thus able to cease splitting operations in 1982 at two more junctions, Swanley and Faversham. A few peak hour commuter trains from the Maidstone and

Chatham lines still use the LCDR City terminus at Holborn Viaduct, but most City traffic from Kent is handled at Cannon Street, Thanet services using the Chislehurst loops to join the SER main line.

Fast services in Kent are scheduled for Class 411 (4CEP) operation, but there is considerable common use of Class 423 units, even on boat trains. No trains on the South Eastern Division now have refreshment cars. When electrification took place in 1959/61 semi-fast and stopping services were worked by Class 414 (2HAP) units and some of these remain in Kent, despite the lack of corridor connections and full access to lavatory facilities for such long journeys as Victoria to Ramsgate. Other Class 414 stock can be found on the Central Division coastal services which during 1982 were formed into four coach units and reclassified as Class 413 (4CAP) units, and on the South Western Division, where they have enabled 12 and 8-car trains to be reduced respectively to 10- and 6-car formations.

Boat trains are an important aspect of South Eastern Division activity with services from Victoria in connection with Sealink sailings from Dover and Folkestone to Ostend, Dunkerque, Calais and Boulogne. Catering today mainly for the holiday traveller and itinerant youth this traffic has considerable seasonal variations. There is none of the traditional glamour about present day boat trains, which are indistinguishable from EMU formations bound for Margate and Ramsgate, except for the addition sometimes of a motor luggage van (Class 419) for mails and registered baggage. Only the 'Venice-Simplon-Orient Express' train two or three times a week provides a replica of past Pullman splendour. Two new forms of cross-channel travel are also catered for; special trains from Victoria are run in connection with the Belgian Jetfoil service from Dover to Ostend, while passengers for the Hoverspeed flights from Dover to Calais and Boulogne are conveyed by the ordinary fast trains from Charing Cross to Dover Priory. As for the Channel Tunnel, the habitual negative attitude of British governments to this project has probably delayed any possibility of completion within the present decade.

The main line electric stock in use on the SR has almost all been built since 1959 and with the normal thirty year mechanical and electrical life of Southern electric vehicles the question of major replacement should not arise during the 1980s. Refurbishment on the lines of the Class 411 programme may be needed to bring the interior layouts and fittings of the 1960s up to the standards and tastes of future years. The Class 414 sets however are no longer suitable for main line work because of their lack of through access. Similar and contemporary units on the ER are currently being refurbished, but many of the Class 414s have been downgraded temporarily to suburban duties in the past and this may well become their permanent fate.

South Western Division

Bottom left: Standing under the vast glass roof of Waterloo station, Class 50 No 50.033 *Glorious* cools off after arriving with the 06.26 service from Exeter on a cold and snowy 11 December 1981. The snow can still be seen on the locomotive's front. *Colin Marsden*

Above: If, due to operating difficulties on the WR a Class 50 locomotive is not available for the Waterloo-Exeter service, motive power substitution may occur. Normally a Class 33 or 47 is provided but if these are not readily available other power may be used. This was the case when Class 31 No 31.423 was photographed at Waterloo on the 19.10 Exeter service early in 1982. *M. Lawrence*

Above right: Refurbished Class 50 No 50.031 *Hood* accelerates away from the 40mph restriction at Clapham Junction and heads towards Clapham Cutting with the 11.10 departure from Waterloo on 11 January 1982. During this decade speed restrictions will be raised with projected realignment of the station. *Colin Marsden*

Below right: In this view of Wimbledon West looking south, the four South Western running lines can be seen on the right, whilst the two on the left are the Central Division Wimbledon-Croydon via Morden lines. Traversing the SWD up main line Class 50 No 50.047 *Swiftsure* heads the 07.35 Exeter service towards Waterloo on 5 May 1981. *Colin Marsden*

9

Right: The 1981/2 winter was particularly bad for the SR with heavy snowfalls both before and after Christmas, necessitating the curtailment of many services. Filling in for a Class 50, Class 33 No 33.004 heads the 09.10 Waterloo-Exeter past Wimbledon on 11 January 1982. *Colin Marsden*

Below: To improve passenger comfort on the Waterloo-Salisbury-Exeter route, Mk II stock that was displaced by IC125 train sets on the WR, were introduced on the SR West of England route from early 1980. Headed by unrefurbished Class 50 No 50.026 *Indomitable* the 13.00 departure from Waterloo passes New Malden on 5 March 1980. *Colin Marsden*

Bottom: Surbiton lies some $12\frac{1}{2}$ miles from Waterloo in the heart of suburbia. Storming out of the cutting at the London end of the station with the 11.10 Waterloo departure is Class 50 No 50.049 *Defiance*. At this point on the journey west the train would be travelling at between 80-90mph. *Colin Marsden*

Above: The quadruple tracks of the SWD main line between Waterloo and Basingstoke see almost equal amounts of traffic traversing both local and main lines. Approaching Walton-on-Thames Class 33 No 33.024 works the 06.50 Yeovil Junction to Waterloo train on 28 March 1981. *Colin Marsden*

Above left: Following a decision to introduce Class 50 2,700hp locomotives on the Waterloo-Exeter route from the early 1980s, a major driver training programme had to be undertaken. Prior to the introduction of the Type 4 service, one train in each direction was Class 50 operated each day for this purpose. No 50.042 *Triumph* passes West Byfleet station with the 06.15 Exeter-Waterloo service on 8 April 1980. *Colin Marsden*

Below left: The first scheduled stop on the Waterloo-Exeter route is Woking, some 25 miles from Waterloo which is covered in 26 minutes. Applying the air brakes for the Woking stop on 15 May 1981 No 50.043 *Eagle* brings the speed down from the 90mph maximum allowed for the stretch of line covered. *Colin Marsden*

Above: To the west of Woking is the deep tree-lined cutting of St Johns, emerging from here on 27 August 1980 is refurbished Class 50 No 50.019 *Ramillies* at the head of the 07.37 Exeter-Waterloo. During the Class 50 refurbishing programme whenever possible it was preferred to operate refurbished locomotives on this service as a higher reliability level was ensured. *Colin Marsden*

Below: Departing from Waterloo at 10.10, 12.10 and 14.10 are locomotive hauled services on the Waterloo-West of England route that terminate at Salisbury. Some of these services are formed of TC stock, but the 14.10 departure still retains a Mk I coaching stock formation. The 14.10 from Waterloo passes Bramshot near Fleet, headed by Class 33 No 33.007 on 9 April 1981, while on the up local line a car train from Eastleigh to the ER is headed by a Class 47. *Colin Marsden*

Top: The last 'up' service from Exeter via the LSWR route terminates at Basingstoke where connection with a Bournemouth-Waterloo service is made. Class 33 No 33.028 stands at Basingstoke after arrival with the 19.55 (now 20.20) Exeter service.
Andrew French

Above: The old order of the Waterloo-Exeter route, with power being provided by Class 33 locomotives. It was for only a short period during 1980 that the Class 33s were used on the service hauling trains of Mk II stock. The 1V09 09.00 Waterloo-Exeter service is photographed near the now closed station of Oakley on 15 April 1980.
Colin Marsden

Right: At the majority of stations on the SR the old goods sheds and yards have been removed or sold to private enterprise. However at Andover the railway goods shed has survived into the 1980s and was still in regular use during 1980. The 11.00 departure from Waterloo headed by Class 33 No 33.017 makes ready to depart from Andover on 15 April 1980.
Colin Marsden

Below: Following the demise of other more interesting classes of diesel locomotive such as the Class 52s and 55s many enthusiasts turned their attention to the lower powered Class 33s. Photographed at Salisbury after a heavy rainstorm on 19 January 1980, Class 33 No 33.020 awaits a crew change on the 17.55 Exeter-Waterloo. *Andrew French*

Left: Following the take over of the Salisbury-Exeter section by WR during the 1960s, the majority of the route was singled, and some of the lesser used stations closed. Templecombe illustrated here closed on 7 March 1966, however the platforms still remain, and during 1982 attempts were made to reopen the station. Indeed on three successive Sundays during September of that year the Basingstoke-Paignton service made a special stop there. Class 47 No 47.466 passes the weed covered platforms on 29 June 1981 at the head of the 13.10 Waterloo-Execer service. From the introduction of the 1983 summer service the station is again timetabled for a regular, but infrequent service. *Colin Marsden*

Below: Approaching Vauxhall, the first station out of Waterloo, a 12-car formation of Class 491/430 (TC/REP) stock forms one of the hourly semi-fast services to Bournemouth. During the 1982/3 timetable these services were booked to cover the 108 miles from Waterloo to Bournemouth in 136 minutes. *John Glover*

Left: Although the SR operates a sizeable fleet of de-icing trains, when heavy snow and prolonged icy conditions prevail the third rail electric units tend to suffer many failures, mainly due to ice forming on the live rail, inhibiting power collection. Occasionally diesel locomotives are required to assist emu trains in these conditions and on 9 January 1982 Class 33 No 33.025 *Sultan* was photographed hauling an emu formation on a Portsmouth-Waterloo service near West London Junction. *Colin Marsden*

Below left: For the majority of inner and outer suburban duties on the SWD, Class 423 (4VEP) and Class 421 (4CIG) units are used. Departing from Surbiton with a Guildford-Waterloo via Woking train 4VEP No 7743 leads another unit of the same class. Although the maximum speed of these units is 90mph this is not often reached whilst operating on suburban duties. *Colin Marsden*

Above right: After leaving Surbiton the line progresses south towards Woking and the first point of major importance is Hampton Court Junction, where the branch line to Hampton Court and the Guildford via Cobham line diverge. Approaching the junction signal Class 423 (4VEP) No 7823 operates the 11.22 Waterloo-Portsmouth stopping service on 24 January 1980. *Colin Marsden*

Right: Perhaps the only trains conforming to emu requirements that can really be described as 'mainline' power are the Class 430/491 (REP/TC) formations which operate between Waterloo/Bournemouth/Weymouth; the total power output of the Class 430 (REP) units is 3,300hp, equal to that of the now extinct Class 55 'Deltic' locomotives. With the REP unit leading, an up semi-fast service accelerates away from the Basingstoke stop passing the village of Basing. *Colin Marsden*

Left: It is more than likely that during the course of the 1980s the stock on the Waterloo/Bournemouth/Weymouth line will be replaced, and 1980s style emu formations based on the Class 455 units are probably the type to be built. Accelerating away from Winchester Class 430 (4REP) No 3002 heads the 11.02 Bournemouth-Waterloo on 7 July 1981. *Colin Marsden*

Right: At the beginning of the 1980s much of the remaining semaphore signalling in use in the Southampton area was replaced by modern computer controlled signals of the multi-aspect colour light type. One major landmark that disappeared at the beginning of 1982 was the signal gantry spanning the Fareham lines at St Denys. Being propelled by a Class 430 (REP) two Class 491 (TC) units start to decelerate for the severe bend into Southampton as they pass St Denys with the 14.45 service from Waterloo on 7 July 1981. *Colin Marsden*

Below: Much of the countryside between Southampton and Bournemouth forms part of the New Forest, providing some very attractive country settings for the railway photographer. Class 491 (4TC) No 402 heads a down Waterloo-Bournemouth/Weymouth fast service near Beaulieu Road. On arrival at Bournemouth the two trailer units are hauled on to Weymouth, while the tractor awaits to haul the next service back to London. *John Vaughan*

Right: Between Bournemouth and Weymouth the trains are operated by Class 33/1 locomotives, operating in multiple with the trailer units, trains being hauled in the down direction and propelled in the up, the Class 33/1 remaining at the back and being driven from the remote cab of the TC unit via the 27 wire Westcode control system. Here No 33.104 heads for Weymouth near Wool hauling a single trailer set. *John Vaughan*

Below: A daily spectacle during the summer months is the arrival and departure of the Waterloo boat train at Weymouth Quay hauled by a Class 73 as far as Bournemouth, where a Class 33/1 locomotive takes over for the journey through to Weymouth Quay, including operation through the public streets between the town and quay stations. To meet DOE requirements the Class 33/1 locomotives are fitted with an electrical socket on their nose ends where a flashing light and bell unit is attached for use while operating through the streets. No 33.102 is shown here working the 16.00 service bound for Waterloo with lamp and warning bell attached. *Chris Davis*

Above: The Portsmouth main line from Waterloo diverges from the Bournemouth and Salisbury line at Woking, after travelling through the town of Guildford the line winds its way towards Hampshire. Forming one of the hourly semi-fast services from Waterloo to Portsmouth Harbour, Class 421 (4CIG) No 7414 passes Milford on a dull 7 June 1982. *Colin Marsden*

Above left: At the London end of Havant station the LSWR Portsmouth route joins the LBSCR line from Brighton, now forming the 'Coastway' line. A down semi-fast service formed of Class 423 (4VEP) stock approaches the junction and slows for the 30mph speed restriction on 12 June 1982. It is unlikely that any rise in this speed restriction will occur during the 1980s. *Colin Marsden*

Below left: The supply of some emu trains and crews for the Portsmouth area is provided by a sizeable shed and depot at Fratton, $1\frac{3}{4}$ miles the London side of Portsmouth. However over 50% of the services operated in the area are worked by drivers and guards who are allocated to other depots. Class 421 (4CIG) No 7408 passes Fratton station with the depot behind, while working the 17.48 Waterloo-Portsmouth Harbour fast service during the summer of 1982. *Colin Marsden*

South Eastern Division

Left: On the South Eastern Division main line between Charing Cross and Hastings, services are operated by demus. These trains formed of six-car sets were first introduced during 1957 to replace steam hauled services. Class 201 (6S) No 1001 hurries past Chelsfield station with one of the hourly Hastings-Charing Cross trains on 4 June 1982. *Colin Marsden*

Above: One of the most famous trains of all time was the 'Night Ferry', the only train that brought continental passenger stock to the BR system in recent years, and was withdrawn on 30 October 1980. For many years the regular motive power for this train was Class 73 electro-diesels, and on 25 July 1980 only a few months before the service was suspended, No 73.140 hauls the up 'Night Ferry' near Polhill. *Rodney Lissendene*

Right: Descending the 1:143 bank from Polhill tunnel Class 201 (6S) No 1005 heads towards Dunton Green while working an afternoon Charing Cross-Hastings train. These 25-year old units will be up for replacement during the 1980s or if Government investment is forthcoming the route will be electrified. Either way the units should not be in operation after 1987 as they have blue asbestos insulation and removal of all trains containing blue asbestos has to be undertaken by that date. *Colin Marsden*

Right: Stable motive power for passenger trains on the electrified SED main line system since the late 1950s has been the 4CEP/BEP emus later classified by BR as 411/410. Climbing away from Tonbridge towards Hildenborough with a stopping train from Ashford to Charing Cross during June 1982 is refurbished Class 411 No 411.599. *Colin Marsden*

Below: After departing from Tonbridge trains travel along the comparatively level and straight section towards Ashford. Fortunately for the photographer there are several overbridges on this section giving good photographic vantage points. Class 410 (4BEP) with its buffet out of use, forms an Ashford-London slow service near Marden. *Colin Marsden*

Left: The docks at Folkestone and Dover provide a constant flow of boat trains to and from London, usually these are of 12-car formations of Class 410/411 units, with additional luggage space provided by a Class 419 (MLV) Motor Luggage Van. A boat train from Folkestone Harbour to Victoria is illustrated here headed by Class 419 No 68003 near Headcorn during the summer of 1981. *Colin Marsden*

Below: For many slow and outer-suburban services operating within the confines of the SED, a sizeable fleet of Class 414 (2HAP) units are allocated to Ramsgate. Unit No 6104 approaches Staplehurst while working a Margate-Charing Cross via Canterbury West train on 15 May 1980. *Colin Marsden*

Top: During the 1980s a refurbishment programme was carried out on the complete fleet of Class 410/411 units to bring them into line with the required standards for the decade. Unrefurbished unit No 7172 approaches Ashford with a slow service from Charing Cross, unusually formed of 12 coaches. *Colin Marsden*

Above: From Ashford the line travels south-east towards Folkestone and Dover and the first station is Westenhanger, where platforms are of the staggered type. Unfortunately due to low returns this station only has a passenger service during the peak periods. Passing through the station in an up direction is an additional boat train from Folkestone to Victoria headed by Class 411 No 7194 on 2 June 1982. *Colin Marsden*

Above: With the famous white cliffs of Dover as a back cloth refurbished Class 411 No 1529 works a Margate-Dover-Charing Cross train on 3 June 1982. Services on this route are hourly, operating between Charing Cross and Ashford as eight-car formations, here the train is split with one part operating to Margate via Canterbury, and the other via Dover and the coast route. *Colin Marsden*

Below: From the mid-1970s several Class 423 (4VEP) units were allocated to Ramsgate, and are now used haphazardly with Class 411 units on the majority of Kent services. With Dover Western docks' cranes in the background No 7890 works a Margate-Charing Cross train. *Les Bertram*

Above: With an abundance of BR hanging signs, two trains are captured on film carrying the same headcode at Dover Western docks. On the left a Class 411 No 7124 awaits its passengers with a Faversham bound train, while on the right is a Victoria bound boat train headed by Class 419 No 68001.   *John Glover*

Below: Dover Priory station is situated between two tunnels, Priory and Harbour. The station has three platforms with an adjacent carriage siding, often used for stabling stock that has arrived at the Western docks on boat train services. Unrefurbished Class 411 No 7207 is photographed on the 12.44 Dover Priory-Victoria on 20 February 1982. In the background another Class 411 and a 419 are seen in the stabling point.   *Michael Collins*

Below: The junction for the non-electrified Hastings route from the main line is at Tonbridge. Passing a rather interesting half house Class 202 (6L) No 1011 approaches the station with the 08.45 departure from Charing Cross on 20 February 1982. In the background to the right of the demu a Class 414 (2HAP) emu can be seen stabled in the carriage siding. *Michael Collins*

Bottom: At the eastern end of West St Leonards station is Bopeep Tunnel and Junction. It is here that the coastway and main Hastings-Charing Cross line part company. Crossing the pointwork Class 202 (6L) No 1017 approaches the station with the 12.44 Hastings-Charing Cross on 4 August 1982. If investment is made in this line and electrification goes ahead this lovely old signalbox and semaphore signalling will disappear. *Colin Marsden*

Left: Another station on the SED between two tunnels is St Leonards Warrior Square, situated between Hastings and Bopeep tunnels. Although the six-car demus are always referred to as 'Hastings' units, the section of line between Bopeep Junction and Ore is electrified, as part of the 'Coastway' line. Pulling out of Hasting Tunnel Class 202 (6L) No 1012 arrives in Warrior Square station with a Hastings-Charing Cross train. *John Vaughan*

Above right: Perhaps not considered as a main line by today's standards is the section between Swanley and Ashford via Maidstone East. The line sees little freight traffic, except for a few perishables trains to and from Dover, and the passenger service is two per hour in each direction. A Maidstone-Victoria service climbs away from Borough Green & Wrotham and heads towards Kemsing on 15 May 1980. *Colin Marsden*

Below right: The line between Maidstone and Ashford passes through some very pleasant scenery in the Bearsted, Hollingbourne and Harrietsham area. Class 423 No 7892 is shown here near Hollingbourne while working the 14.36 Victoria-Ramsgate on 27 July 1982. *John Faulkner*

Below: The majority of stations on the Maidstone-Ashford section remain unspoilt, many still retaining original buildings and with semaphore signals still in use. Class 414 (2HAP) No 6123 approaches Lenham with a local service for Ashford on 15 May 1980. *Colin Marsden*

Right: The other main line operated by the SED is via the North Kent lines to Dartford and then to Faversham, from where there are two routes to Dover, either via Margate or Canterbury East. Travelling through the rooftops near Chatham Class 415 (4EPB) No 5041 forms a Charing Cross-Gillingham service. *Colin Marsden*

Below: At the eastern end of Faversham station lays the junction of the Canterbury East and Margate via Herne Bay lines. The junction and immediate surrounding area are controlled by the signalbox to the right in this picture, showing an eight-car formation of Class 411 units coming off the Herne Bay line, with a Ramsgate-Victoria train. *John Glover*

Left: Canterbury East, like many stations in the area, still retains a manual signalbox and this example is of particular interest mounted on iron legs. A Dover Priory-Victoria train slows for the station stop formed of unrefurbished Class 411 No 7187 on 15 August 1981. With various resignalling plans it is quite likely this signalbox will not see the decade out. *John Glover*

Below: Continuing on from Canterbury towards Dover the line passes through two significant mining areas of Snowdon and Tilmanstone, both generating a sizeable amount of freight traffic. Parked in station sidings at Shepherds Well a Class 09 shunter awaits its next trip along the Tilmanstone branch. Class 423 No 7773 approaches with a Victoria-Dover Priory service. *John Glover*

Central Division

Right: Although at Clapham Junction the Central and South Western Divisions run alongside each other from Pouparts Junction, there is no physical connection for trains. Taking the CD main line towards Wandsworth Common Class 421 (4CIG) No 7434 leads a Victoria-Littlehampton service. *John Faulkner*

Below: From Clapham Junction the CD main line heads south through Wandsworth Common towards Streatham Common and East Croydon. In this view a Class 420 (4BIG) four-coach buffet unit approaches Streatham North Junction with a Victoria-Brighton semi-fast service. The two main lines are to the left and the local suburban lines to the right, however if due to operating problems one of the lines is blocked, fast services may use the slow lines or vice-versa. *Colin Marsden*

Left: The four track line continues to Coulsdon North, where the Quarry and Redhill lines diverge, joining back together at the north end of Earlswood Station. Crossing from the down Redhill line to the down fast at Earlswood are three 3-car demu units led by Class 207 (3D) No 1305 working a London Bridge-Redhill-Eastbourne service. Services on this route are normally emu operated but to balance stock the 09.25 service from London Bridge is diagrammed for demu operation. *John Faulkner*

Below: One of the main hubs of railway activity on the CD is Gatwick Airport where many thousands of air travellers pass through each day, and during the late 1970s special accommodation was provided for passengers' luggage on this route. During 1984 new stock is to be introduced on the Victoria-Gatwick service formed of Mk II air braked coaches powered by Class 73 locomotives. One of the extra luggage space-fitted Class 427 (4VEG) units departs from Gatwick bound for Victoria on 18 May 1982. *Brian Morrison*

Left: A London Bridge-Redhill-Brighton train formed of Class 421 (4CIG) No 7394 moves slowly over a 20mph speed restriction at Tinsley Green, south of Gatwick Airport. Above the rear two coaches of the train the remains of the original Gatwick Airport station, closed in 1958, can be seen. The present station is sited on the former racecourse station. *Colin Marsden*

Below: The four track section continues on from Gatwick to Three Bridges where two lines diverge to Horsham, the other two continuing to Brighton via Balcombe. A twelve car formation of Class 421/420 (4CIG/BIG) stock passes Balcombe with a Victoria-Eastbourne service on 22 March 1980. At the time this photograph was taken the original Southern concrete style lamp standards still existed. *John Faulkner*

Left: A scene that cannot be repeated. This view of Balcombe Tunnel Junction taken during 1980 shows the signalbox and junction layout, both removed during 1981, when signalling came under the control of Three Bridges and the 2 to 4 track junction re-positioned half a mile to the London side. Class 421 No 7404 heads a Littlehampton-Victoria train. *John Vaughan*

Right: One of the photographic highlights of the CD London-Brighton main line is the portal of Clayton Tunnel, looking more like a fort than a railway tunnel. Pulling out of the London end Class 421 (4CIG) No 7311 forms a Brighton-Victoria semi-fast service on 28 April 1982. Clayton Tunnel is 1 mile 499 yards in length. *Colin Marsden*

Above: Having completed some $47\frac{1}{2}$ miles from Victoria a Littlehampton bound service approaches Patcham Tunnel to the north of Preston Park, headed by Class 421 (4CIG) No 7334. On this secton of the line there are some five trains in each direction per hour giving the photographer plenty of scope, but alas 99% are formed of emu stock. *Michael Collins*

Left: Branching off from the London-Brighton main line at Keymer Junction to the south of Wivelsfield is the secondary main line to Lewes, and on to Seaford and Eastbourne. Passing the signalbox at Lewes, which undoubtedly will be replaced before the decade is out, is Class 423 No 7840 forming an Eastbourne-Brighton service. *John Faulkner*

Below left: At the southern extremity of the CD Brighton line operating area are three major terminal stations, at Brighton, Seaford and Eastbourne, all receiving heavy passenger flows in the holiday season. Passing the carriage sidings on the left and approaching Eastbourne, Class 420 (4BIG) No 7044 arrives with a service from Victoria. *Colin Marsden*

Above right: At Three Bridges the Mid-Sussex line diverges from the main Brighton line and passes through Crawley and Horsham to Ford where it joins the Brighton-Portsmouth Coastway line. Passing the now disused platforms of the old Crawley station Class 421 (4CIG) No 7370 works the 10.14 Horsham-Victoria service on 22 February 1982. *John Faulkner*

Bottom right: Although the majority of services traversing the Three Bridges-Horsham section are from London to the south coast, there are hourly trains that terminate at Horsham. After arrival with a down service it is necessary to make a shunt to gain access to the up line platform. It was during one of these shunt movements that Class 423 (4VEP) No 7723 was captured on film. *Colin Marsden*

Bottom far right: The terminus at Bognor Regis is quite an impressive station with four platform roads and adjoining carriage siding. Departing from the station with a Mid-Sussex line service for Victoria is Class 423 (4VEP) No 7870. Two trains per hour operate on this service, one being semi-fast and starting from Portsmouth Harbour, the other being a slow service starting from Bognor Regis. *John Vaughan*

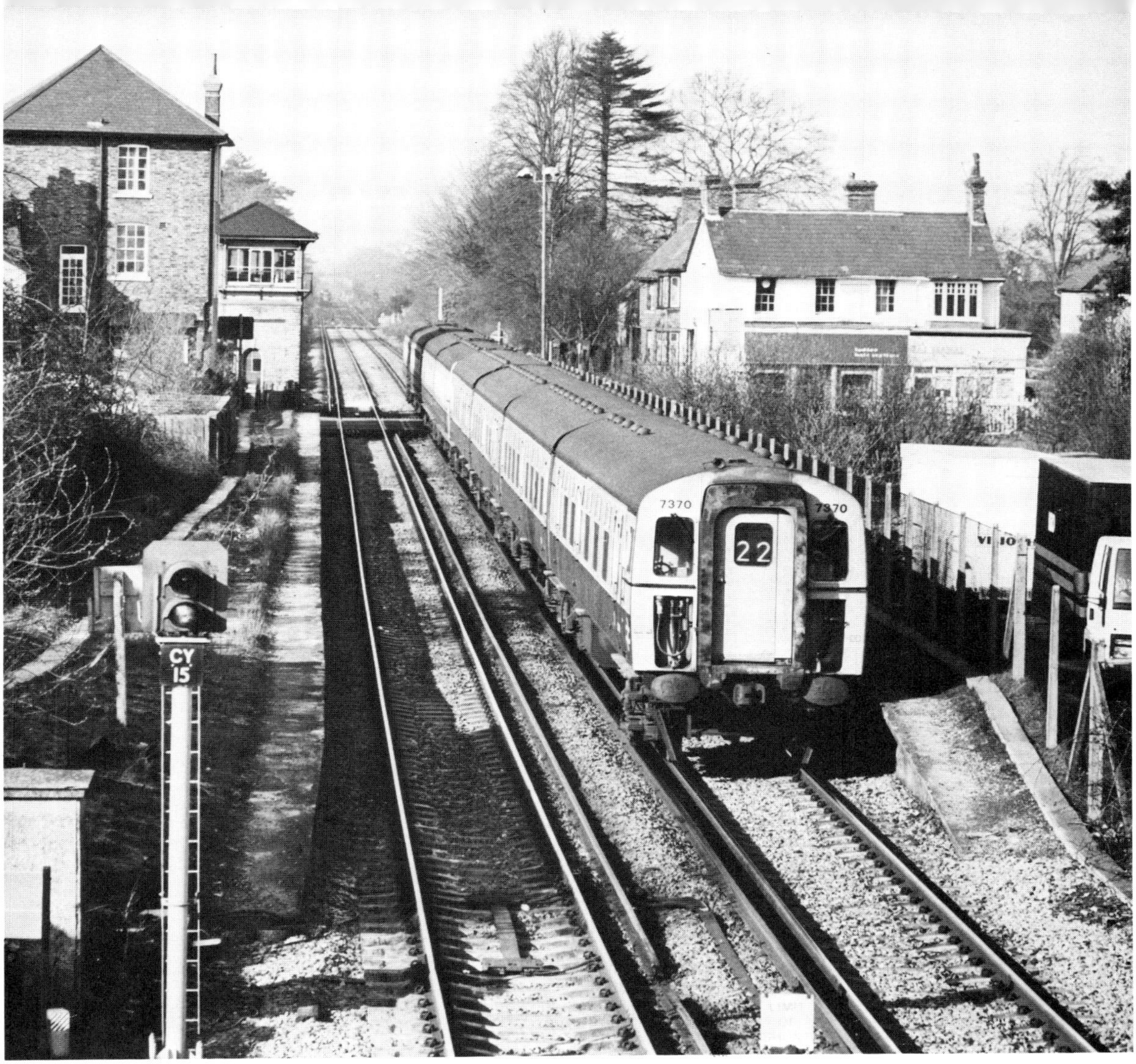
7370
7370
22
CY
15

7723
7723
22

56

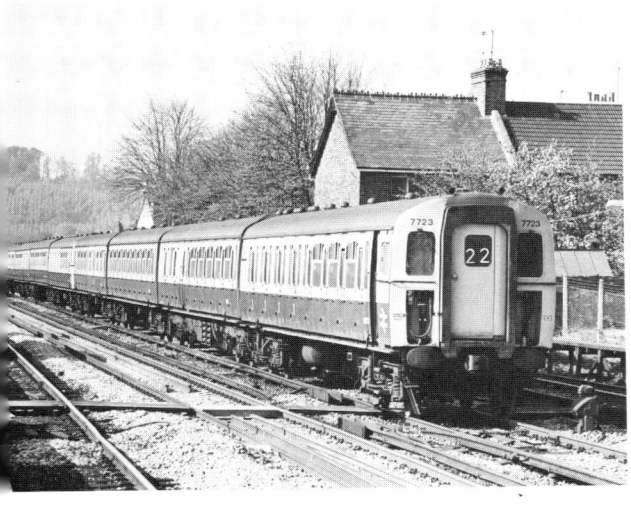

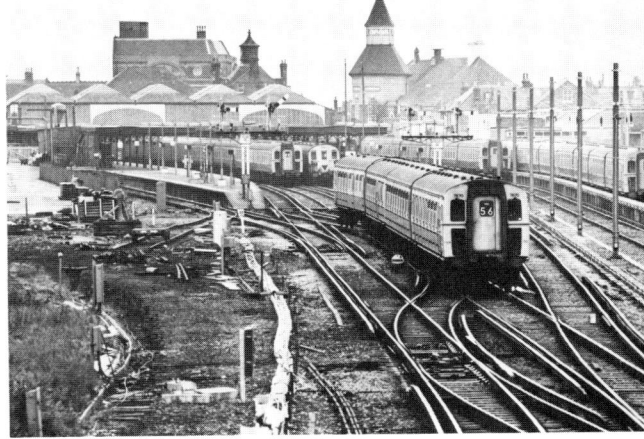

Venice-Simplon-Orient-Express

The following seven pictures have been included to show the most luxurious train to operate on the SR since the demise of the 'Brighton Belle' during the early 1970s. The train is formed of Pullman cars privately owned by the Venice Simplon Orient Express Ltd, a part of the Sea Containers Group, and operates three days a week between London Victoria and Folkestone, and commenced on 28 May 1982. At Folkestone Harbour passengers travel on the BR ferry to Boulogne and then continue their journey to Paris, Milan and Venice by preserved continental Pullman and sleeping car vehicles. On British soil the train is normally headed by a Class 73 locomotive carrying the distinctive VSOE headboard. Prior to the commencement of the service several dummy and test runs were operated for timing and crew training.

Above left: One of the trial trips on 5 May is pictured here passing Bickley Junction hauled by Class 73 No 73.142 *Broadlands. Colin Marsden*

Bottom left: With the dream train in tow Class 73 No 73.136 accelerates away from Tonbridge on 4 June 1982 with the 11.44 Victoria-Folkestone Harbour. The train is routed via Brixton, Herne Hill, Beckenham Junction, Petts Wood, Sevenoaks, Tonbridge and Ashford. *Colin Marsden*

Top right: Normally the train is formed of seven Pullman cars and a former LNER baggage car, and although the train is scheduled to depart from Folkestone Harbour at 16.00hrs it is often delayed depending upon late arrival of the boat or delays in unloading. Class 73 No 73.124 passes Cheriton near Fokestone West with the up train on 3 June 1982. *Colin Marsden*

Centre right: The northbound train operates on Thursdays with the southbound service the following day, so considerable empty running is unavoidable as the stock is kept and maintained at Stewarts Lane. Passing the now closed platforms of Folkestone East Class 73 No 73.142 slows to cross into Folkestone East yard to gain access to the harbour branch. *Colin Marsden*

Bottom right: Between Folkestone East and the harbour the train is operated with a locomotive at each end. Slowly traversing the branch, Class 73 No 73.124 leads the empty stock into Folkestone Harbour for the 16.00 departure, with sister locomotive No 73.142 on the rear. *Colin Marsden*

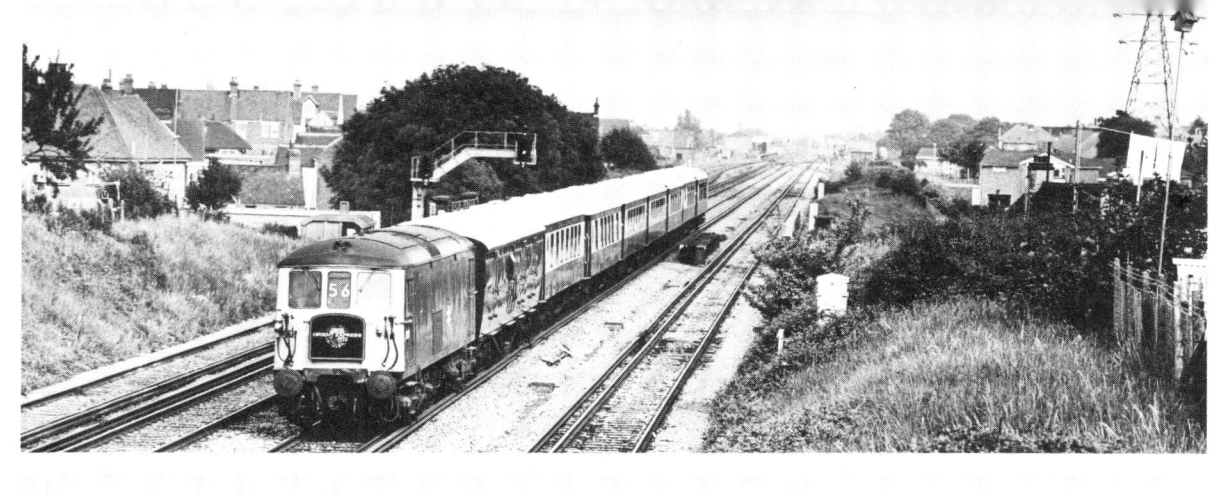

Above: With locomotives attached to both ends the VSOE awaits is passengers at Folkestone Harbour. It is interesting to note that the locomotive operating the train to London conveys the headboard on the buffer stop end of the train on the harbour branch, due to the reversal at Folkestone East. *Colin Marsden*

Below: Immaculate Class 73 No 73.142 *Broadlands* takes the strain of the VSOE as it departs from Folkestone Harbour. Whilst covering the 72 miles to Victoria in 96 minutes passengers are served with tea. A single passenger ticket for the return Victoria-Venice trip with food would cost £500. *Colin Marsden*

Inter-Regional Workings

The principal axis of inter-regional traffic is via Reading and Basingstoke, once served by the GWR Birkenhead and the LNER Newcastle to Bournemouth through trains. Their present day successors are respectively: two services from Liverpool and one from Manchester to Poole and trains from Derby and Newcastle to Poole. All these run via Birmingham, Oxford and Reading, where they reverse and Class 47 locomotives are the normal motive power south of Birmingham. The Newcastle-Poole train is formed of Mk II air-conditioned stock and was the first regular working of this stock on to the SR.

A few years ago the use of IC125s on this route was mooted but financial restrictions on the size of the IC125 fleet now makes this unlikely. The daily services mentioned above are duplicated at summer weekends and some trains are extended to Weymouth. The growing traffic on this route has also required the introduction of two Sunday services in each direction. An innovation in 1982 was a new service from Manchester to Portsmouth running via Reading, Guildford and the Portsmouth Direct line. This routing avoids reversal at Reading and taps a new source of traffic at the important junction and university town of Guildford.

The only inter-regional services to pass through the London area are the twice-daily Manchester-Gatwick-Brighton trains which run via Kensington Olympia. The Saturday night/Sunday morning southbound train is routed via the WCML to Willesden Junction, but the remainder take the WR route from Birmingham via Oxford and Reading to Old Oak Common, again with Class 47s providing the motive power. This is a revival of the LNWR and LMS 'Sunny South Express' with the difference that its passengers are bound not for the beaches of Sussex but for the Mediterranean sunshine to be reached by flights from Gatwick Airport.

The second important inter-regional route is from Portsmouth and Southampton via Salisbury to Bristol and Cardiff. An interval service of twelve trains daily runs as far as Bristol and the number of intermediate stops has been reduced to bring the Southampton-Bristol journey time down to around 100 minutes. Motive power on this route has experienced frequent changes since the SR Moguls and WR 'Halls' disappeared, but currently most trains are worked by SR Class 33 locomotives, which use this service as a link to their new fields of activity in South and West Wales and along the Welsh border. On Saturdays one of the trains runs through from Brighton to Cardiff, while a second through service from Brighton runs via Salisbury to Exeter, extended to Paignton during the summer, and has the distinction of double-headed Class 33 haulage.

Below: Perhaps the SR has the least number of inter-regional workings but nevertheless those that do arrive bring a variety of motive power and a change from the steady flow of emu trains. The CD Brighton lines see two through inter-regional trains daily to and from Manchester, normally powered by Class 47 locomotives. The 07.30 Manchester-Brighton traverses the down fast line at Salfords headed by **Class 47 No 47.450 on 9 March 1982.** *Colin Marsden*

Above: The afternoon Brighton-Manchester service departs at 15.00hrs with its first stop at Gatwick Airport therefore providing an excellent connection for air passengers with the Midlands. The journey then continues via Clapham Junction, West London line to Old Oak Common, and on to Reading, Oxford and Birmingham. Class 47 No 47.463 leads the 15.00 Brighton-Manchester service through Balcombe station on 22 March 1980. *John Faulkner*

Below: Several changes in inter-regional services have occurred during the early 1980s mainly the replacement of aged Mk 1 coaches with modern Mk 2 types, with some services from the north-east now operated by air conditioned Mk 2D/E/F vehicles. Departing from Basingstoke taking the Reading branch is Class 33 No 33.007 at the head of the 10.23 Poole-Manchester on 16 August 1980. *Andrew French*

Above: Motive power for the majority of inter-regional passenger services is provided by Class 47/4 locomotives fitted with electric train heating. However up to the end of 1982 some steam heat fitted examples were still to be found. Class 47 No 47.148 with the 09.42 Poole-Manchester climbs away from Winchester towards Wallers Ash on 7 July 1981. *Colin Marsden*

Above left: Most inter-regional trains work on a north-south axis, arriving on the SR at Basingstoke from Reading but originating from places such as Derby, Liverpool, Leeds, Manchester and Newcastle. The goods/passenger loops of Wallers Ash can be seen in the background as Class 47 No 47.459 heads towards Wallers Ash tunnel on 3 August 1980. *Colin Marsden*

Below left: After arrival on Southern metals the majority of Table 51 services only call at Basingstoke, Southampton and Bournemouth, with some services working forward to Weymouth. Racing through Eastleigh Class 47 No 47.483 is in charge of a Liverpool-Poole train on 7 July 1981. *Colin Marsden*

Top right: Through inter-regional services from the north still convey buffet cars, but for how many more years remains to be seen. A nine-car formation of mainly Mk 2 stock, except for the BG and buffet car, pass Beaulieu Road forming the 09.10 Manchester-Weymouth headed by Class 47 No 47.032 on 6 August 1982. *Michael Collins*

Below right: A considerable amount of inter-regional passenger traffic is generated by excursions or special trains. Each year up to 25 specials operate from all over the country to Spalding for the flower festival. The SR usually operate two or three specials to this one event. The 1980 festival on 10 May saw Class 47 No 47.556 on a special from Portsmouth Harbour, seen here approaching Woking junction. *Les Bertram*

Below: When specials operate from the LMR or ER it is usual practice for the Southern to power the train from Brent, Willesden or Kensington Olympia. On 19 June 1982 a special from Bolton worked to Hastings and the SR provided Class 33 No 33.060 to relieve from the 25kV AC electric locomotive at Mitre Bridge. The train is illustrated here on the Ashford-Hastings line at Rye. *M. Lawrence*

Above: Another source of inter-regional traffic to SR are BR or privately sponsored railtours. A very popular BR tour was on 17 October 1981 when the 'Wessex Deltic' Railtour from Finsbury Park to Bournemouth, Eastleigh and Portsmouth was headed by Class 55 No 55.015, seen in the illustration approaching Eastleigh. *Colin Marsden*

Below: Many hundreds of enthusiasts turned out on 7 July 1982 to travel on the DAA 'Grid Iron Grice' Railtour from London Bridge to London Bridge via the Midlands. Motive power was Class 56 No 56.014 and the train is seen here passing Forest Hill on its outward journey. The operation of specials such as this are extremely complex as both locomotive and crews have to be specially drafted in from another region. This was the first occasion that a Class 56 had been used on a passenger train on SR. *Colin Marsden*

47

Commuter Services

Many of the 260,000 commuters conveyed by the Southern Region in and out of London every day travel on the main lines but much of the region's mileage is composed of secondary routes and branches which handle little else but commuter traffic, particularly since the decline in local freight traffic. Some of the commuter routes extend 40 miles or so from London, deep into the stockbroker belt.

The South Western Division includes two of these outer suburban lines; Waterloo to Reading serving the select localities of Sunningdale and Ascot as well as the new town of Bracknell, and Waterloo to Guildford via Cobham with its secluded executive estates interspersed by unspoilt open country. Both routes are provided with first class accommodation on their trains and when the 4COR sets were withdrawn from the Reading line in 1972 their replacement was with main line Class 421 (4CIG) stock. Speeds on the Windsor line out of Waterloo are restricted; the peak hour services run non-stop to Staines or beyond but off-peak trains now make a number of intermediate stops so that the company car on the M3 offers an attractive alternative.

On the New Guildford line via Cobham first class travel was reintroduced in 1973 after a lapse of 32 years and during peak hours with four trains running per hour the normal Class 423 (4VEP) units are strengthened by second class only EPB stock of classes 415 or 416. Fast main line running between Waterloo and Surbiton keeps journey times down on this route. The branch from Pirbright Junction to Alton is served normally by portions detached from main line trains at Woking, but during the rush hours separate through trains, both semi-fast and stopping, run between Waterloo, Farnham and Alton, formed of Class 423, 421 and 414 (4VEP/4CIG/2HAP) stock. Other stopping trains terminate at Woking during the peak hours, supplementing the half-hourly Waterloo-Guildford (direct) service.

The 26-mile 48 minute journey to Windsor places this branch geographically outside the inner area but it is served by semi-fast trains normally formed of suburban EPB stock. Railborne tourists to Windsor probably favour the Western Region's 26 minute IC125 connection via Slough but the SR terminus at Riverside retains facilities for handling special excursions and Royal trains, though the former royal waiting rooms are now in private occupation. In contrast the other stations on the branch are unstaffed and have fallen into a state of disrepair.

Another intermediate route is that between Epsom, Leatherhead, Dorking, Horsham and Effingham Junction. Although the area is up-market in status and rural in scenery, apart from a few peak-hour Mid-Sussex line trains from Victoria, it is operated by second class only stopping trains from both Waterloo and Victoria making cross platform interchange at Epsom. To cater for commuter traffic to the housing estates between Raynes Park and Epsom the normal half-hourly service from Waterloo is increased to a 10 minute frequency but even limited stop trains have to follow the pace of stopping services on the slow lines out of Waterloo. Stations between Dorking and Horsham are only served during rush hours and the 31 miles to Warnham, for example, takes about an hour from either Waterloo or Victoria.

The group of inner suburban routes from Waterloo comprises the branches to Chessington, Hampton Court and Shepperton, the Kingston Roundabout and the Hounslow Loop. Since 1981 most off-peak services have been operated by Class 508 units, to be replaced from 1983 by the SR designed Class 455 stock, with the help of EPB stock and Class 405 (4SUB) units, mainly during peak hours.

The Shepperton branch has three peak hour semi-fast trains each way via Richmond, but otherwise the rush hour services within the inner suburban area provide few additions to the basic half-hourly frequency. During weekday evenings and on Saturdays the Roundabout service operates only between Waterloo and Kingston via Richmond. The least used of these routes is the Hounslow Loop which traverses a semi-industrial area and is subject to competition from the Piccadilly tube. Its Sunday trains narrowly escaped withdrawal in 1981 but a limited hourly service was retained. The inner London stations of Vauxhall and Earlsfield are not served by most Epsom and Shepperton line trains, but in contrast to their equivalents on the Central and South Eastern Divisions they remain open during the late evenings.

The Central Division suburban area extends as far as Epsom Downs, Tattenham Corner, Caterham and Coulsdon North. Epsom Downs and Tattenham Corner stations were built with numerous platforms and extensive sidings to cater for race traffic but these facilities have now been drastically rationalised. Epsom Downs once had regular through trains to both Victoria and London Bridge but is now served only by a circuitous half-hourly train to Victoria via West Croydon on weekdays only.

The twin branches to Tattenham Corner and Caterham, splitting at Purley, still enjoy four services per hour during the peak periods but after the morning rush, stations on the Tattenham Corner line are unstaffed and a conductor issues tickets to the few passengers boarding the two-car trains. Peak hour and some late evening trains terminate at London Bridge but off-peak services on Mondays to Fridays continue to Charing Cross, a reminder that these branches were originally SECR property. The 23 miles from Charing Cross to Tattenham Corner takes an hour by through train; peak hour trains starting from London Bridge with fewer stops reach Tattenham in about 45 minutes but late evening services calling at all stations except Penge West require 15 minutes longer.

On Saturdays the through trains to Tattenham and Caterham are covered by a Charing Cross-Redhill service via Sydenham which also replaces the Monday-Friday London Bridge-Redhill trains via Tulse Hill. Formed of main line Class 423 (4VEP) stock these trains provide occasional first class service within the inner suburban area. During weekday rush hours some of the Redhill trains are extended to Reigate, giving a very limited electric service on this first stage of the line to Reading. The substantial station at Coulsdon North, once the terminus of AC electrics from Victoria, is now only open during Monday to Friday peak hours, mostly for limited stop trains to Victoria. The station is due for closure as part of the Brighton line resignalling scheme and the site redeveloped; its services will be replaced by additional trains to nearby Smitham on the Tattenham Corner branch.

The Central Division operates the Region's only diesel commuter service over the Oxted line to East Grinstead and Uckfield. A route which has several times missed electrification, its links with the South Coast were cut during the 1950s and 1960s and it exists now only as a London commuter line with hourly DEMU departures, at present from London Bridge but normally from Victoria, to each destination splitting at Oxted. Augmented rush hour services include some Class 33 hauled trains to and from London Bridge.

The remaining suburban routes of the Central Division can be described as a series of concentric circles linking Victoria and London Bridge with radial lines extending to East Croydon and Epsom. The pattern of service is complex and is made more bewildering to the stranger by variations between the peak hour, off-peak, Saturday and Sunday routes. During the Victoria resignalling and air terminal construction works many peak hour and weekend trains start and terminate at Clapham Junction.

Certain links have very limited services; in 1982 only five trains (SX) traversed the spur between Tulse Hill and Leigham Junction (Streatham Hill) and there is only a sparse peak hour service from London Bridge to Crystal Palace via Sydenham. After 20.00 many of the London Bridge services are reduced to hourly operation and several of the lesser-used stations are closed during the late evening. The South London line, the first to be electrified by the southern companies, is now limited to a Monday-Friday operation with many of its trains terminating at Battersea Park instead of Victoria.

A link with the South Eastern Division is provided (SX) by the Holborn Viaduct-Tulse Hill-Selhurst-West Croydon service, but during peak hours this reverts to the pre-1978 route Holborn Viaduct-Tulse Hill-Wimbledon-Sutton which serves all three divisions. Wimbledon to West Croydon is a fascinating cross-country single line served on weekdays by half-hourly two car (Class 416) trains which pass on the double track through Mitcham Junction; at some stations tickets were sold from the signalboxes.

The EPB stock on the Central Division was the first to benefit from refurbishment of its Class 415 and 416 units, the division also operates the remaining Class 418 (2SAP) sets and a dwindling number of Class 405 (4SUB) units, including the eye-catching No 4732 restored to Southern Railway malachite green livery.

Traffic within the inner area is declining rapidly, services are being cut back and the LBSCR legacy of substantial Victorian buildings is subject to vandalism and decay, for which the current remedy is a drastic reduction to bus-stop facilities. In the outer residential areas of scattered housing and high car ownership (such as the Tattenham branch) services are often slow and unattractive while the inner suburban lines built to carry armies of clerks to City offices are now surrounded by a cosmopolitan population employed, if at all, in a variety of manufacturing and service industries.

The South Eastern Division's suburban services are based on the original LCDR and SER routes. The former run from Victoria, Holborn Viaduct and Blackfriars to Orpington via Herne Hill and to Sevenoaks via the Catford Loop and Swanley. Holborn Viaduct station closes after 19.30 on **Mondays to Fridays so late evening trains start from** Blackfriars and do not call at the lesser-used stations, while at weekends the whole of the LCDR City branch is closed and all trains run to and from Victoria. Operation of mixed main line, boat train, suburban and freight traffic over the section from Victoria to Brixton has been improved by the new connections installed in 1982 enabling Catford Loop line trains to take the little-used South London line (now termed the Atlantic Line) between Wandsworth Road and Peckham Rye.

The more extensive SER system radiates from Charing Cross and Cannon Street, though the latter terminus also closes after 19.30 and all day at weekends. In addition a few peak hour trains depart from Holborn Viaduct and Blackfriars to the Dartford lines via Nunhead and Lewisham. On the Mid-Kent line all trains now run to Hayes, with a connecting two-car shuttle on weekdays from Elmers End to Addiscombe, mainly for the benefit of staff based at the stabling depot there. Another shuttle runs uncertainly at peak hours from Elmers End to Selsdon and Sanderstead, a little used service whose long-postponed closure is drawing near. The

Below: Undoubtedly the most unique section of BR is the 1½ mile long Waterloo & City line linking Waterloo with Bank and City of London. The line currently carries some 17,000 people in each direction per day and is therefore one of the heaviest-used commuter lines in the country. A five-car formation with car S52 leading pulls out of the carriage sidings at Waterloo on 26 August 1981.
Colin Marsden

frequency and variety of services available at East Croydon has attracted commuters away from this end of the Mid-Kent line with its slow and roundabout route to London.

On the SER main line suburban services run as far out as Sevenoaks (22 miles), though late evening operation is now cut back to Orpington. At Grove Park these connect on weekdays with a shuttle service to Bromley North, but during peak hours some through trains run from Charing Cross to this branch.

The Dartford group of lines comprises four routes: via Greenwich and Woolwich, via Blackheath and Woolwich, via Bexleyheath and via Sidcup (the Dartford Loop). Two trains per hour run semi-fast calling at Lewisham, Woolwich Arsenal, Abbey Wood (for Thamesmead new town), Dartford and Gravesend to Strood and Gillingham (Kent) — 36 miles and 68 minutes from Charing Cross. Two stopping trains hourly run as far as Gravesend and the remaining services terminate at Dartford. During the rush hours many of the extra trains terminate at Crayford, Barnehurst or Slade Green, according to the route taken, and proceed thence to the South Eastern Division's major stabling and servicing depot at Slade Green.

The basic service frequency on the South Eastern Division since the timetable reorganisation of 1976 has been every 20 minutes, in contrast to the half-hourly services on the other two divisions, but this **extra provision is a likely target for economy cuts.**

The chronic overcrowding of South Eastern services during the early post-war years was relieved by the operation of 10-car trains in peak hours in and out of Charing Cross and Cannon Street, following an extensive programme of platform lengthening and track alterations during the 1950s. Consequent on the general decline in commuter traffic and lack of investment in new rolling stock, from the winter service of 1982/83 many ten-car trains were reduced to eight allowing the extra Class 416 (2EPB) units to replace non-standard Class 405 (4SUB) stock on the other divisions. The South Eastern Division has been operated entirely by standard EPB stock for a number of years.

Despite shorter trains the suburban routes still receive quite a generous peak hour service with the standard twenty minute frequency from Charing Cross being duplicated by a similar service from Cannon Street, plus short workings to Sidcup etc, and the Holborn Viaduct/Blackfriars trains. On the other hand the South Eastern Division is probably the worst affected by cancellations due to staff shortage.

Below: With the introduction of flexible working hours in many spheres of employment, the period of commuter trains can be spread over a wide time scale. Workers from places such as Windsor, $25\frac{3}{4}$ miles from Waterloo start to depart from their home stations from about 6am and consequently commence the homeward journey any time after 14.30 hours. Departing from Platform 14 at Waterloo Class 423 (4VEP) No 7821 forms a Waterloo-Windsor & Eton Riverside service during 1980. *Colin Marsden*

Top: Of the three SR divisions the SWD has the widest variety of types of units, and as well as using the wellknown suburban classes of 405, 415, 416 and 508, utilise some of the main line class 414, 421 and 423 trains. With an eight-car formation formed of four 2-cars an up Chessington-Waterloo service passes West London junction (Queenstown Road). *Colin Marsden*

Above: Many additional services operate on the SR during peak periods. Forming a rush-hour service from Reading, Class 423 (4VEP) No 7852 traverses the four track Waterloo-Windsor line section approaching Wandsworth Town, during early 1980. The four track section continues as far as Barnes. *Colin Marsden*

Right: An interesting comparison of modern high density rolling stock with, on the left a BR designed and built Class 508 emu, and on the right LTE designed but Metropolitan Cammell built D stock. Although built by different companies both have destination indicators, front end emergency doors, headlight, marker lights, tail lights and an automatic coupling. *Colin Marsden*

Above: Much of the commuter stock used on SR dates back to the early 1950s and by the late 1970s was scheduled for replacement. However with low investment levels no purpose built stock was available until 1982. To tide the region over a fleet of 43 Class 508 units initially intended for the LMR were allocated to the SR. No 508.029 leading an eight-car formation is seen here near Raynes Park with a Hampton Court-Waterloo commuter service. *John Faulkner*

Below: For many years the Central and South Western Divisions have used the 30-year old Class 405 (4SUB) units on many of their commuter services and inner suburban lines. In recent years with the reorganisation of rolling stock it has become possible for units to be used on a more restricted basis. No 4633 departs from Surbiton with a slow service for Waterloo on 11 May 1980. *John Faulkner*

Above: Numbers of Class 405 units have been diminishing gradually in the early 1980s finally disappearing from the suburban scene from mid-1983, being replaced by purpose built Class 455 high density units. A four-car Class 405 No 4296 stands at Epsom station with a Victoria-Effingham train on 30 May 1981. *Colin Marsden*

Right: Effingham Junction on the New Guildford line is also served by trains from Waterloo/Victoria via Epsom, a half-hourly service from alternate stations. The service via Epsom arrives just ahead of the Waterloo-Guildford service so as to provide a connection for Guildford, for those joining the branch service between Motspur Park and Bookham. On a snowy 10 January 1982 Class 508 No 508.007 awaits to depart from Effingham for Waterloo via Epsom. *Colin Marsden*

Above: Many daily commuters to Waterloo live in the pleasant town of Guildford, Surrey some 30 miles from London. Two train services are provided to Waterloo, the main line route and the New Guildford line via Cobham. Class 415 (4EPB) No 5104 departs from Guildford and heads for Guildford London Road station with a Cobham service on 8 July 1981. *Colin Marsden*

Below: The town of Windsor is blessed by having two stations, one operated by the SR and the other by WR. Through services operate to London from the SR station whereas there is only a shuttle service to and from Slough from the WR station. However many regular commuters have opted in recent years to travel via the WR route as shuttle connects with a IC125 service at Slough and London can be reached in a little over 20 minutes, whereas the Waterloo service takes 51 minutes. Class 415 (4EPB) No 5119 stands in SR Windsor & Eton Riverside station with Windsor Castle in the background on 27 May 1981. *Brian Morrison*

Top right: The six-mile Shepperton branch, diverging from the Kingston roundabout line at Shacklegate Junction near Strawberry Hill carries a considerable amount of commuter traffic, with the normal half-hourly service to London via Kingston being supplemented by additional services during peak periods, both via Kingston and the Strawberry Hill and Twickenham route. After departing from Fulwell Class 508 No 508.030 heads towards Hampton on 5 March 1982. *Colin Marsden*

Below right: Commuter services on the SED are mainly formed of Classes 415, 416 EPB type units with the occasional use of Class 414 (2HAP) sets. The traffic radiates from Charing Cross, Holborn Viaduct and Cannon Street. Class 415 No 5192 runs into Waterloo East on 8 May with an Orpington bound train. *Les Bertram*

Below: The section of line between Blackfriars and Holborn Viaduct passes through the centre of one of London's largest office block areas and the size of the train is dwarfed by the overpowering buildings. Class 415 (4EPB) No 5196 painted in modern 'Inter-City' livery departs from Holborn Viaduct and heads for Blackfriars with a Sevenoaks bound train on 13 September 1982. *Brian Morrison*

Top: A modernisation scheme undertaken during the late 1970s was the rebuilding of London Bridge Station, the complete reorganisation of surrounding tracks, and the implementation of a modern power signalbox, all to improve passenger services for the 1980s. Passing under the modern station footbridge during the summer of 1982 is Class 415 (4EPB) No 5222 on a Charing Cross-Addiscombe train. *Colin Marsden*

Above: South east of London Bridge lays a maze of junctions where the South London and New Cross Gate lines diverge from the main SED arterial route, a little further on is the junction for the North Kent line at North Kent East Junction near New Cross. The 'main' line carrying on through New Cross and St Johns still carries a considerable amount of traffic and during peak periods trains operate with a 1½-2 minute headway. Passing New Cross station with the 17.59 Charing Cross-Gillingham on 5 August 1981 is an eight car formation of EPB stock. *Brian Morrison*

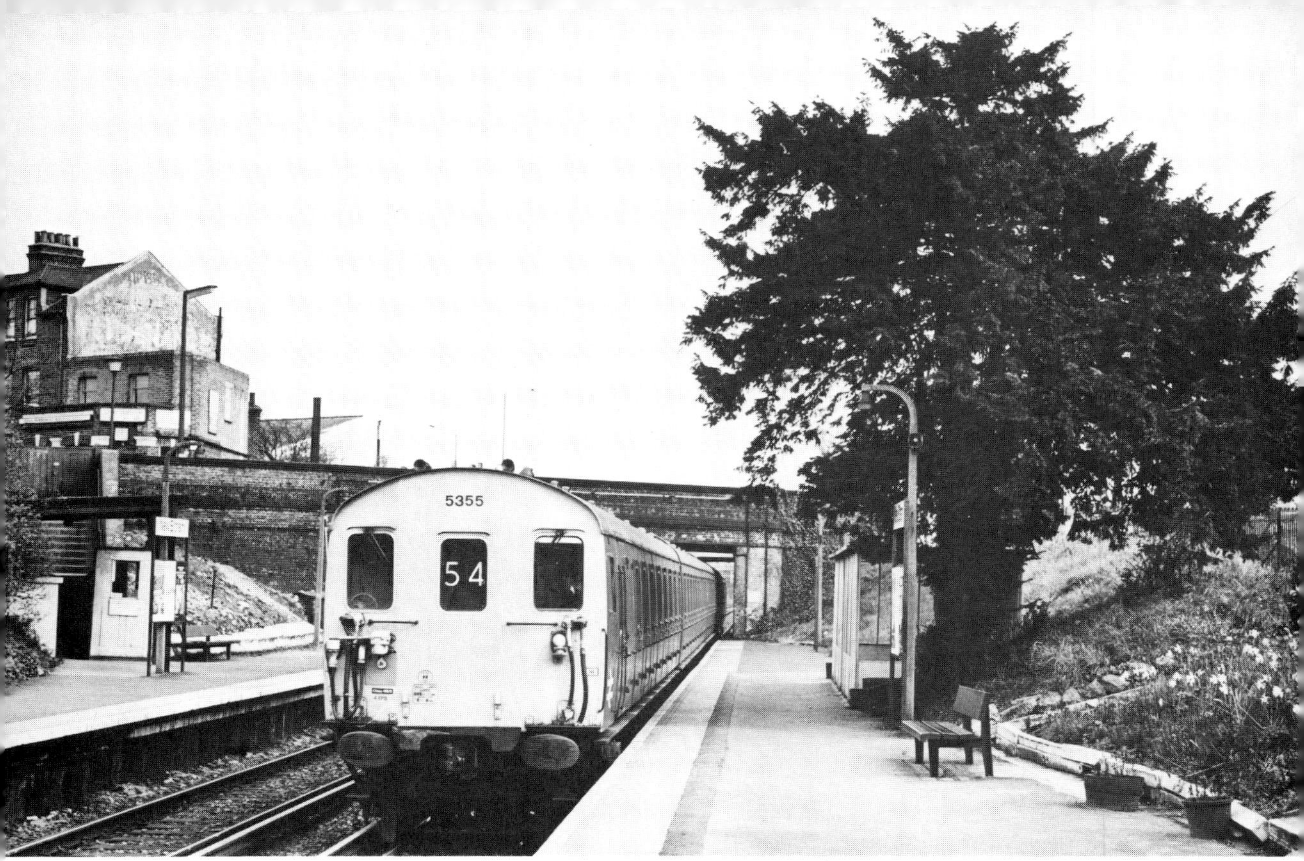
5355
54

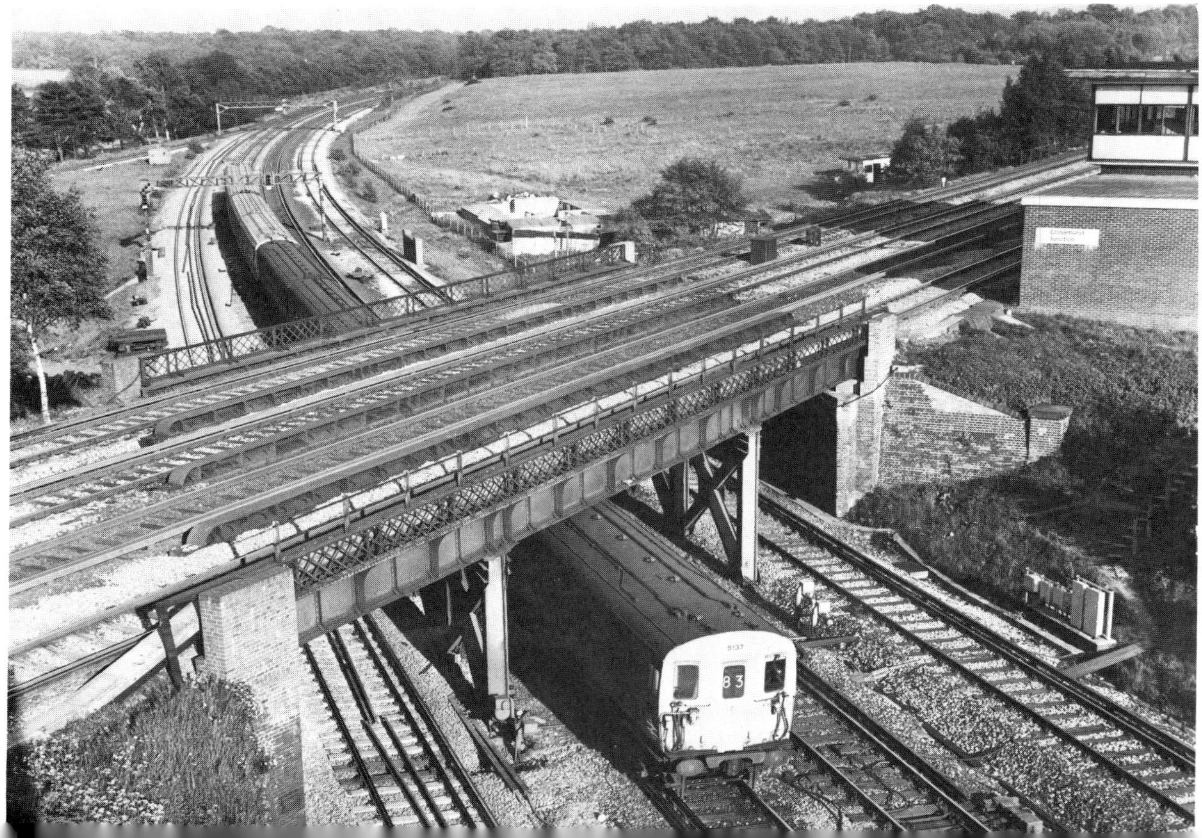
83

Left: From London there are three routes to Dartford, Kent, **an** area from where some 45% of commuters travel daily. The usual route to London is via the Dartford Loop covering the large residential areas of Bexley, Sidcup and Eltham. Approaching New Eltham station with a Dartford–Charing Cross train is BR designed Class 415 (4EPB) No 5355. *Colin Marsden*

Below left: Between Chislehurst and Petts Wood is a very complex junction layout where the SED main Hither Green and Sevenoaks line is crossed by the London–Swanley via Bromley line. At this point both four track sections have full interconnecting access. In this view the actual crossing of the Hither Green–Sevenoaks line is seen above the Bromley–Swanley section, with Class 415 (4EPB) forming a Sevenoaks–Holborn Viaduct via Swanley train. *Brian Morrison*

Right: During recent years many of the now ageing emu **fleet** have been repainted in standard 'Inter-City' blue and grey livery giving a more pleasing appearance. Passing through the deep cutting at the London end of Chelsfield station Class 415 (4EPB) No 5309 slows for the station stop while working a Charing Cross–Orpington–Sevenoaks train on 4 June 1982. *Colin Marsden*

Below: The SED suburban fleet is largely allocated to Slade Green depot, situated on the North Kent line to Dartford. The depot not only provides stabling and maintenance facilities for up to 200 coaches, but has a full workshop where major repair work can be undertaken. BR designed Class 415 (4EPB) No 5354 arrives at Slade Green on 6 February 1982 with a Gillingham–Charing Cross service. *Colin Marsden*

Right: Many commuter services terminate at Dartford but a sizeable number continue on through North Kent to Gravesend and Gillingham. Departing from the somewhat basic platform amenities at Greenhithe SR designed Class 415 (4EPB) No 5186 forms a Cannon Street-Sidcup-Gravesend train on 29 May 1981. *Colin Marsden*

Below: Higham station some 30 miles from Charing Cross is not one of the best served stations in Kent with only an hourly off peak service. However during the 07.00-09.00 peak period no fewer than eight trains stop at the station in the up direction. With Higham tunnel in the background Class 416 (2EPB) No 5715 stops with a Gillingham-Charing Cross service. *John Faulkner*

Above: Clapham Junction just outside London's Waterloo and Victoria (CD) stations is the hub of daily commuter traffic with many passengers using the station as an inter-divisional link between the SWD and CD. A packed Southern commuter service of the early 1980s formed of 30 year old Class 405 (4SUB) stock pauses on the up Central Division local platform with a train from East Croydon to Victoria. *Colin Marsden*

Left: The CD commuter lines after passing Clapham Junction continue through Wandsworth Common towards Balham where the line to Streatham Hill diverges, and the main line continuing on through Streatham North junction towards Streatham Common. Traversing the down local track towards Streatham North Junction an eight-car formation of Class 418 (2SAP) units led by No 5615 works a Victoria-Coulsdon North duty on 4 March 1982. *Colin Marsden*

61

Right: During off peak periods emus are berthed and cleaned at Streatham Hill in addition to the maintenance facilities provided at nearby Selhurst. Class 405 (SUB) No 4679 passes the carriage sidings at Streatham Hill while working a train from Victoria to Epsom Downs via Crystal Palace. During peak periods trains on this section of line are on average every 10 minutes, whereas in off peak times trains are four per hour. *Colin Marsden*

Below: At Crystal Palace the lines divide, with one route (high level section) continuing to Sydenham Junction and eventually New Cross, while the low level lines, with a frequent passenger service goes to Bromley Junction, where services can either be routed on to Beckenham Junction, or via Norwood Junction to either the CD main line or the West Croydon branch. Crystal Palace high level now sees little passenger use, except during peak periods. Passing through the station, now devoid of its overall roof, Class 421 (4CIG) No 7374 works empty stock from Stewarts Lane to New Cross. *Michael Collins*

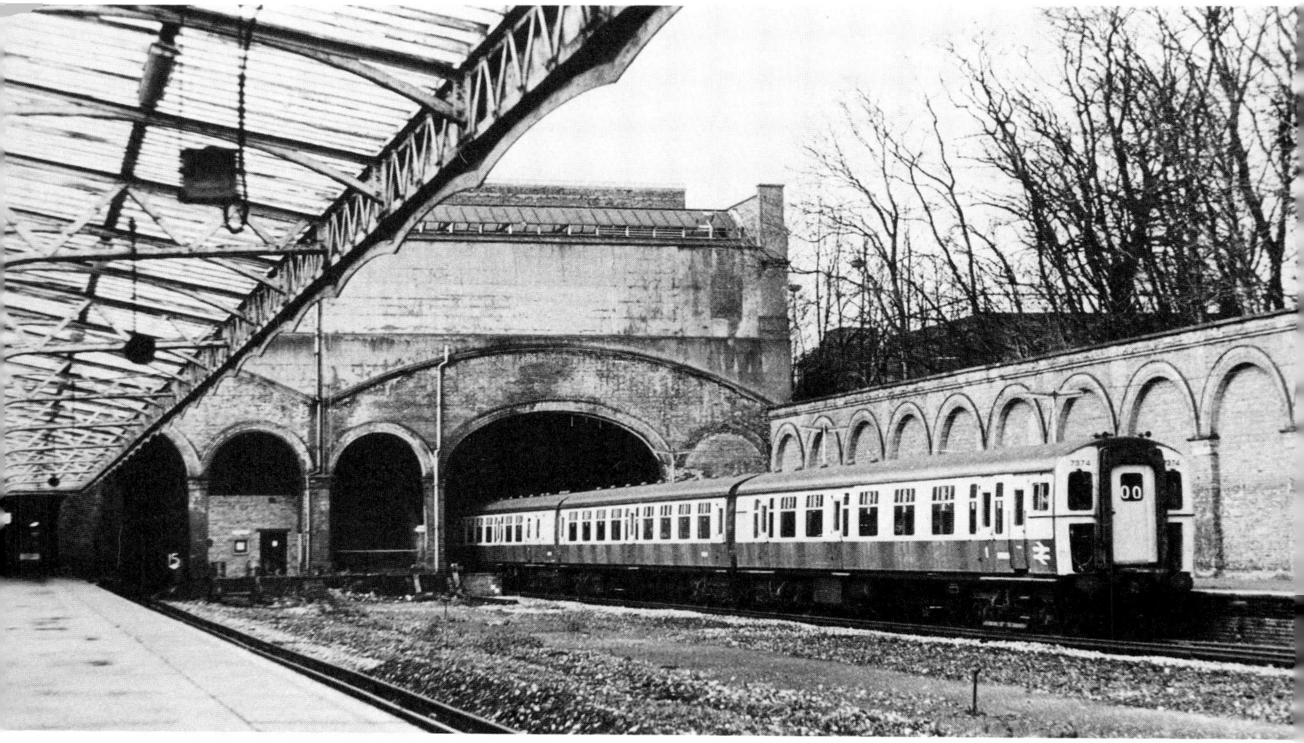

Above: The CD suburban line to Coulsdon North has been much in the news during the early 1980s with its closure imminent following track rationalisation as part of major track and signalling work in the area. When the station eventually closes passenger traffic will be transferred to Smitham on the Tattenham Corner branch. Class 405 (4SUB) No 4674 arrives at Coulsdon North on 24 September 1980 with the 16.54 service from London Bridge. *Les Bertram*

Below: The line from West Croydon to Wimbledon is a single line with passing places, worked with a single line staff until 24 May 1982 when the line came under the control of the new Victoria power signalbox (at Clapham Junction) thus replacing all the semaphore signalling with modern colour lights and a tokenless block single line system. Departing from Waddon Marsh Class 416 (2EPB) No 5656 passes an array of semaphore signals while heading for Wimbledon. *John Glover*

Top right: It is obvious that when Tattenham Corner station was built in 1901 the SECR envisaged great potential for the station probably from the nearby Epsom Downs racecourse. However the line now only sees a half-hourly service with few additionals during peak periods. In this view of the four platform station an assortment of Class 415/416 (4 and 2EPBs) can be seen. *Brian Morrison*

Below right: The commuter line between Epsom and Horsham is served jointly by SWD and CD trains. During off peak periods SWD trains run alternate half hours to Dorking and Effingham Junction, with the CD providing the corresponding service. During peak periods some Waterloo trains are extended to Horsham, whereas the CD service is provided throughout the day. Stations between Dorking and Horsham are closed at off-peak times. Four Class 418 (2SAP) units descend Holmwood Bank on a Victoria-Horsham train in this illustration. *John Vaughan*

Below: The non-electrified lines of the CD commuter system to East Grinstead and Uckfield are operated by demu sets of Classes 205 and 207. During off-peak periods trains run from London to Oxted as six-car formations from where the front three coaches continue to Uckfield and the rear three to East Grinstead. During peak periods services from London operate to both branches. Class 207 (3D) No 1317 nears Crowhurst while working the 10.17 service from London Bridge to East Grinstead. *Colin Marsden*

Top left: In peak periods to supplement the demus between London and East Grinstead and Uckfield, a few locomotive hauled formations operate, hauled by Class 33s with a rake of Mk 1 coaches. Locomotives rostered to these duties are allocated to Hither Green, enabling 'slim-line' Class 33/2s to be used. Class 33/2 No 33.202 stands in one of the bay platforms at London Bridge on 5 March 1981 with the 18.18 service to East Grinstead. *Martin Searle*

Below left: Occasionally due to inter-divisional workings Eastleigh allocated locomotives operate the loco-hauled commuter services. This was the case on 3 July 1980 when No 33.028 was captured on film working the 17.34 London Bridge-East Grinstead service out of East Croydon. It is likely that these services will be replaced by dmu formations in the near future. *Les Bertram*

Below: In the 1982/3 timetable there were three up East Grinstead loco-hauled trains in the mornings departing at 07.25, 08.01 and 08.27, covering the $30\frac{1}{2}$ miles in 52, 56 and 59 minutes respectively. Passing the wooden signalbox at Oxted a Class 33/0 slows for the station stop during the early 1980s. *John Vaughan*

Branch Lines

A number of branch lines still exist within the region; some of them built as such and others which have recently reverted to branch line status following discontinuance of through services. The current policy is to reduce the number of junctions where trains have to be joined and separated and at only seven stations is this now carried out regularly — Woking, Gatwick Airport, Barnham, Eastbourne, Purley, Oxted and Ashford.

Within London's outer suburbs the Virginia Water to Weybridge link used to be served by half-hourly Waterloo-Windsor/Weybridge trains splitting at Staines, also by a few peak hour trains to Waterloo via Weybridge. During the off-peak hours on weekdays the branch is now served by three Class 416 trains which shuttle every thirty minutes between Staines and Weybridge. The timing of the main line connection from Waterloo at Weybridge makes it impossible to connect with the Reading-Waterloo trains at Virginia Water so that the branch train has to continue to Staines where it connects into the Windsor-Waterloo services. This uneconomic operation probably lies behind the threats of withdrawal of the off-peak services.

Continuing towards Reading, portions for Guildford via Camberley and Aldershot used to be detached from the Waterloo trains at Ascot. For a few lavish years separate trains ran four times an hour from Waterloo with cross-platform interchange between each pair at Ascot. However since 1981 Ascot to Guildford has been worked as a branch outside peak hours, usually with a four car train of Class 421 or 423 stock. Commuters from Frimley and Camberley often find it quicker to drive to Farnborough and join the fast trains on the main line.

A true branch line on the South Western Division is from Brockenhurst to Lymington Pier. Electrified in 1967 it is normally worked by Class 423 or 414 stock, connections are made at Brockenhurst with the Waterloo-Bournemouth semi-fast trains and at Lymington Pier with the ferries to Yarmouth (IoW). On summer Saturdays a few through services run to and from Waterloo and these eight-car trains tax the power supply to the branch so that they have to be driven with their motors coupled in series. The branch is single line worked under One Train block regulations.

The Central Division branches have through services from London or Brighton with the exception of the line from Tunbridge Wells to Eridge. This is the truncated remnant of a once busy cross-country route from Tonbridge to Brighton. Its hourly DEMUs connect at Tonbridge with Charing Cross-Ashford trains, so giving Tunbridge Wells a half-hourly service from London, and at Eridge with the Oxted line DEMUs to Uckfield. The passage of the DEMU every hour is the only activity now at the imposing LBSCR station of Tunbridge Wells West. Without the addition of this service to the Hastings traffic at Tunbridge Wells Central the remedy of singling the line through the station and the narrow tunnels each side would become a possibility.

A non-electrified enclave within the South Eastern Division is the line from Ashford to Hastings worked by a variety of DEMU classes. Long threatened with closure, economies have been made by singling the line between Appledore and Ore leaving a passing loop at Rye, which enables an hourly service to be maintained. With the limited capacity of this line, the necessity to reverse at Eastbourne on the Central Division route and the restrictive loading gauge over the Tunbridge Wells-St Leonards line, Hastings is virtually cut off from excursion traffic.

The South Eastern Division has two former through routes which are now operated as branch lines. Charing Cross-Gillingham trains used to detach at Strood a portion for Maidstone West. Now except for four rush-hour trains from Charing Cross, this operates as a shuttle service from Strood to Paddock Wood with some additional trains between Strood and Maidstone to serve the industrial area of the Medway Valley. At the Paddock Wood end there are also four through trains from Charing Cross via Tonbridge, one of which completes the circuit by returning to Charing Cross via Gravesend. Branch trains, usually formed of suburban EPB stock, connect at Paddock Wood with the Charing Cross-Ashford services.

After electrification in 1959, the Sheerness branch was served by an hourly through train from Victoria via the Sittingbourne Western to Middle Junctions curve, an hourly service all stations from Dover via Faversham, and an hourly shuttle service from Sittingbourne. Together this made an intensive service to operate over this mainly single track branch. Now only the shuttle service remains,

running at hourly intervals for most of the day, and there is one Monday to Friday train each way to Victoria via the curve.

Not quite a true branch line but difficult to describe otherwise is the Isle of Wight section of the SR. Reduced to a Ryde Pier Head-Sandown-Shanklin remnant of the once island-wide system it survives to cater for the seasonal influx of holidaymakers to these resorts as well as carrying a regular commuter traffic. It has the distinction of operating the oldest stock on BR, the ex-London Transport standard stock vehicles of 1923-35 vintage which were purchased for electrification in 1967 and reclassified as Class 485 (4VEC) and Class 486 (3TIS). These veterans continue to receive overhaul and refurbishment but their life cannot be prolonged indefinitely and it is difficult to find newer BR or LT stock which would fit the restricted clearances and also withstand exposure to salt water on the Ryde Pier Head extension.

Above: There are not many true branch lines close to London, however the four daily trains in each direction between Clapham Junction and Kensington Olympia can only be described as a 'branch' service with the morning trains until October 1982 formed of typical 'branch' formation of a main line locomotive hauling two coaches. After that date WR allocated dmus operated the service. Class 33/2 No 33.201 comes off the West London extension line at Clapham Junction with the empties from the morning Clapham Junction-Kensington Olympia trains on 17 August 1981. *Colin Marsden*

Right: During the 1980s a regular half-hourly shuttle service has operated over the Staines-Weybridge branch, although a through London service is provided during the peak periods. Normally Class 416 (2EPB) or Class 508 units operate this working. 2EPB No 5787, one of the South Tyneside built units, approaches Weybridge on 28 March 1981. *John Faulkner*

Above: Many people would consider the line from Ascot to Guildford via Aldershot as a cross-country connection, however in SR's eyes it is classified a branch line. Until the early 1980s the line had through services from London via Ascot, but with the 1981 cutbacks services were restricted to between Guildford and Ascot only on a half-hourly basis. Usually trains are formed of Classes 421, 423, (4CIG/VEP) stock, but when this picture was taken at Camberley on 8 July 1981 the 10.34 service from Guildford was formed of Class 415 (4EPB) No 5112.   *Colin Marsden*

Right: From Brockenhurst there is a $5\frac{1}{2}$ miles branch to Lymington Pier, primarily to serve the ferry to the Isle of Wight. An approximate half-hourly service operates on this line and trains are normally formed of a single Class 414 (2HAP) unit. During early morning a through service from Eastleigh operates to the branch and on summer Saturdays one through service in each direction operates from Waterloo. Class 414 No 6024 stands at Lymington Pier on 9 August 1982.   *Michael Collins*

Below: The section of line between Andover and Andoversford Junction (Cheltenham) via Savernake closed to regular passengers on 11 September 1961, however the section between Redpost Junction (Andover) and Ludgershall remains intact and is used by the MOD with a regular freight service. On 14 February 1981 a railtour visited the branch from Marylebone headed by Class 47 No 47.292 seen here near Tidworth.   *John Vaughan*

Above: The Isle of Wight once boasted a vast railway system, but alas now only 8½ miles remain between Ryde Pier Head and Shanklin. The line is now operated by former LT underground trains purchased by BR in 1967, with the 11 trains maintained at Ryde St Johns Road. Here unit No 485.043 departs from the station with a service for Shanklin, while set No 032 takes a rest in the bay platform line. In the sidings set No 485.041 can be seen leaving the shed. *Colin Marsden*

Below: Only essential maintenance was carried out on the Island since the present stock's introduction, but during 1982 a 'light' refurbishing programme commenced and units began to emerge painted in blue-grey livery and carrying new six digit numbers. Unrefurbished set No 042 approaches Brading with the 12.41 Shanklin-Ryde on 13 June 1982. *Colin Marsden*

Left: Since the reduction of the Isle of Wight railway system to branch line status in 1967 very little station modernisation has been carried out, although some work has been done to the signalling system. The spare motor car No S10 forms the lead vehicle in unit No 031 as it stands at Brading, a station unaltered for the last 40 years and where gas lighting is still in use. *Colin Marsden*

Right: There has been much speculation in recent years that the line would be re-equipped with modern rolling stock but with the present low level of investment this seems unlikely, and if no new stock is found within the decade, closure of the line must be on the cards. Unit No 044 approaches Ryde St Johns Road with a train for Ryde Pier Head on 14 June 1982. *Colin Marsden*

Below: The CD operates a nine-mile branch line from Lewes to Seaford, served by trains to and from Brighton during off-peak periods, and by a handful of through London services at other times. Approaching Southease on 5 September 1981 is Class 414 (2HAP) No 6016 forming a Brighton-Seaford working. *John Glover*

Right: A section of line on the SR which is scheduled for closure in the near future is between Eridge and Tunbridge Wells Central, with the loss of Groombridge, and Tunbridge Wells West stations. Closure notices were posted during the summer of 1982 but public objections were placed with the TUCC, necessitating the line's retention until all the objections are heard in a public enquiry and its findings published. Waiting to depart for Tunbridge Wells Central in the bay platform at Eridge is Class 207 (3D) No 1304 on 13 July 1981. *John Glover*

Below right: The SED operate a $26\frac{1}{2}$ mile railway which can only be described as a branch line between Ashford and Hastings. Between Ashford and Appledore it is double track, but from thereon to Hastings it is a single line with a passing place at Rye. The line is usually operated by three-car demu stock of Classes 205, 207 (3H/D). However until April 1983 one of the former Reading-Tonbridge 'Tadpole' Class 206 (3R) units No 1206 remained in traffic and was sometimes used. Here the 'Tadpole' unit is deputising for the diagrammed set approaching Appledore with the 16.45 Ashford-Hastings on 27 July 1982. *Colin Marsden*

Top left: The journey between Ashford and Hastings takes 50 minutes with seven intermediate stops. If investment in the railways is forthcoming from the Government this section of line will almost certainly be electrified. Class 207 (3D) No 1306 is seen here between Three Oaks and Doleham stations with a Hastings-Ashford train.
John Vaughan

Left: Another branch line operating within the SED is between Paddock Wood and Maidstone West, serving the hop growing areas of Beltring, Yalding, Wateringbury and East Farleigh. Trains are normally formed of Class 414 (2HAP), or Class 415 (4EPB) units. At Paddock Wood the branch line service starts from the down bay platforms and standing here on 5 April 1980 is Class 414 No 6165.
Colin Marsden

Below: The eight-mile electrified branch from Sittingbourne to Sheerness sees an hourly service, based on the productivity of one unit, however during the peak periods a handful of services start from Faversham and one service each day operates to and from Victoria. Crossing the King's Ferry Bridge at Swale, Class 411 No 1529 forms a service from Sheerness to Sittingbourne on 27 July 1982.
Colin Marsden

Cross-Country Workings

From a glance at a map of the Southern Region the cross-country route from Reading through Guildford and Redhill to Tonbridge is immediately evident. This line nearly became a victim of the Beeching axe during the 1960s but was saved by the adoption of bus stop operation and an economical conversion to diesel traction using existing DEMU and EMU stock to form 'Tadpole' 3R units (Class 206). These were replaced in 1980 on the hourly stopping service by WR DMU sets of Classes 117 and 119. At the same time a new fast hourly service was introduced between Reading and Gatwick Airport, calling only at North Camp, Guildford and Redhill, operated by Class 119 three-car units with additional luggage accommodation provided in former buffet and van areas. This links the Western Region via Reading with Gatwick Airport to complement the road service to Heathrow.

Reading-Portsmouth was a well established route in steam days, but the 1967 electrification of the Bournemouth line enforced two changes at Basingstoke and Eastleigh for through travellers. As part of the improvement of the Waterloo-Salisbury service in 1981 the DEMUs from Reading which had hitherto run to Salisbury were diverted to Portsmouth, providing an additional train about every two hours between Basingstoke and Eastleigh. The weekday trains are formed of Class 204 and 205 (3T/3H units) but the Sunday service is worked by Class 33/1 locomotives and TC sets.

Between Portsmouth and Salisbury, in addition to the approximately hourly fast trains to Bristol, there is an hourly limited stop train to either Salisbury or Romsey plus an hourly stopping service as far as Southampton. These are also worked by Class 204 and 205 DEMU stock. Portsmouth to Eastleigh and St Denys are awkward gaps in the South Western Division electrified network and Sunday diversions of Waterloo-Bournemouth trains have to be diesel hauled from Havant to Southampton. The alternative route via Romsey and the new Laverstock curve outside Salisbury (opened in 1981) involves an even longer use of diesel traction between Southampton and Basingstoke.

The coastal lines of the LBSCR from Portsmouth to Brighton and Brighton to Hastings are today marketed under the name of 'Coastway'. Electrified throughout during the 1930s, services have been cut back during recent years. Westward from Brighton there are hourly semi-fast and stopping trains to Portsmouth and a local train to Littlehampton. Connections are made at Barnham and Littlehampton with the stopping trains off the Mid-Sussex route from Victoria.

Eastwards out of Brighton (with no physical contact to the West Coast line) there is a regular 20 minute stopping service as far as Lewes, where one train per hour diverges to Newhaven and Seaford, one terminates at Eastbourne and the third continues through to Ore. The Seaford branch also has a few peak hour trains direct to Haywards Heath, a survival of the once regular service to Horsted Keynes. Seaford also boasts two Monday-Friday commuter services to London, one each to Victoria and London Bridge. Some of the branch trains to Lewes and Brighton form links in Paris-London connections off the Dieppe car ferries.

Rolling stock on the Coastway lines tend to be vintage. Successively 2NOL, 2BIL and 4COR units spent their last years on the coastal routes and they have been followed by Class 414 sets, these now paired with guards/luggage vans adjoining to form Class 413 units.

At the western extremity of the region Weymouth is served by WR cross-country trains from Bristol and Westbury, usually formed of DMUs, but with a few loco-hauled trains, mainly in connection with Channel Island sailings.

72

Above: The major cross-country working originating on SR is the regular service between Portsmouth Harbour and Bristol/Cardiff. These services are normally operated by Class 33 locomotives with rakes of six Mk 1 coaches. Services on this route have been greatly improved during the 1980s. Class 33 No 33.013 approaches Porchester with the 15.10 Portsmouth Harbour-Bristol Temple Meads on 12 June 1982. *Colin Marsden*

Above right: During the early 1980s the Portsmouth-Bristol route was dubbed the 'Wessex line'. After leaving Portsmouth trains traverse the Portsmouth Direct line as far as Portcreek Junction (Hilsea), thence via Fareham to St Denys and the Bournemouth main line as far as Redbridge where the 'Wessex line' diverges to the right and passes through Romsey and on to Salisbury. Passing through St Denys under clear signals Class 33 No 33.013 works the 16.10 Portsmouth-Cardiff on 7 July 1981. *Colin Marsden*

Below right: The frequency of trains is basically hourly through the main part of each day with fewer trains during the early morning, late afternoon and evening. Class 33/1 No 33.102 approaches Southampton with the 11.00 service from Bristol on 25 September 1980. *Colin Marsden*

Right: In addition to the through services between SR and WR a service is provided between Portsmouth and Salisbury formed of demu stock, usually of Classes 204/5 (3T/H). Passing the junction points for Dean Hill Quarry between Dunbridge and Dean, Class 204 No 1403 (formed with the power car from a Class 205 unit) works the 13.07 Portsmouth Harbour-Salisbury on 15 May 1982. *Les Bertram*

Below: During the 1982/3 timetable there were some 12 local services daily each way during weekdays. A Class 205 (3H) with its running number obliterated by snow slowly draws out of Salisbury with a Portsmouth Harbour working during the winter of 1981/2. The demu service stopping at all 19 intermediate stations takes 90 minutes for the $50\frac{1}{2}$ miles journey. *John Vaughan*

Bottom: The cross-country service between Reading and Portsmouth is operated by Classes 204, 205 (3T/H) units on weekdays, but by Class 33/1 locomotives in multiple with Class 491 (4TC) sets on Sundays, usually formed with the locomotive at the Portsmouth end. No 33.101 hauling Class 491 No 419 departs from Mortimer with the 10.00 Reading-Portsmouth on 16 August 1981. *Les Bertram*

Above: The cross-country Portsmouth-Reading service always uses the 'loop' platform at Eastleigh, which is signalled for reversable operation. With Eastleigh works in the background and a Class 73 in the carriage sidings, Class 205 No 1124 departs with a Portsmouth-Reading train on 7 July 1981. *Colin Marsden*

Left: A cross-country service also operates between Reading and Basingstoke, and Basingstoke and Salisbury, again formed of Classes 204, 205 (3T/H) units. Units between Reading and Basingstoke stop at all stations, as do the local services between Basingstoke and Salisbury. Class 205 No 1133 departs from Overton with the 10.25 Salisbury-Basingstoke on 15 April 1980. *John Faulkner*

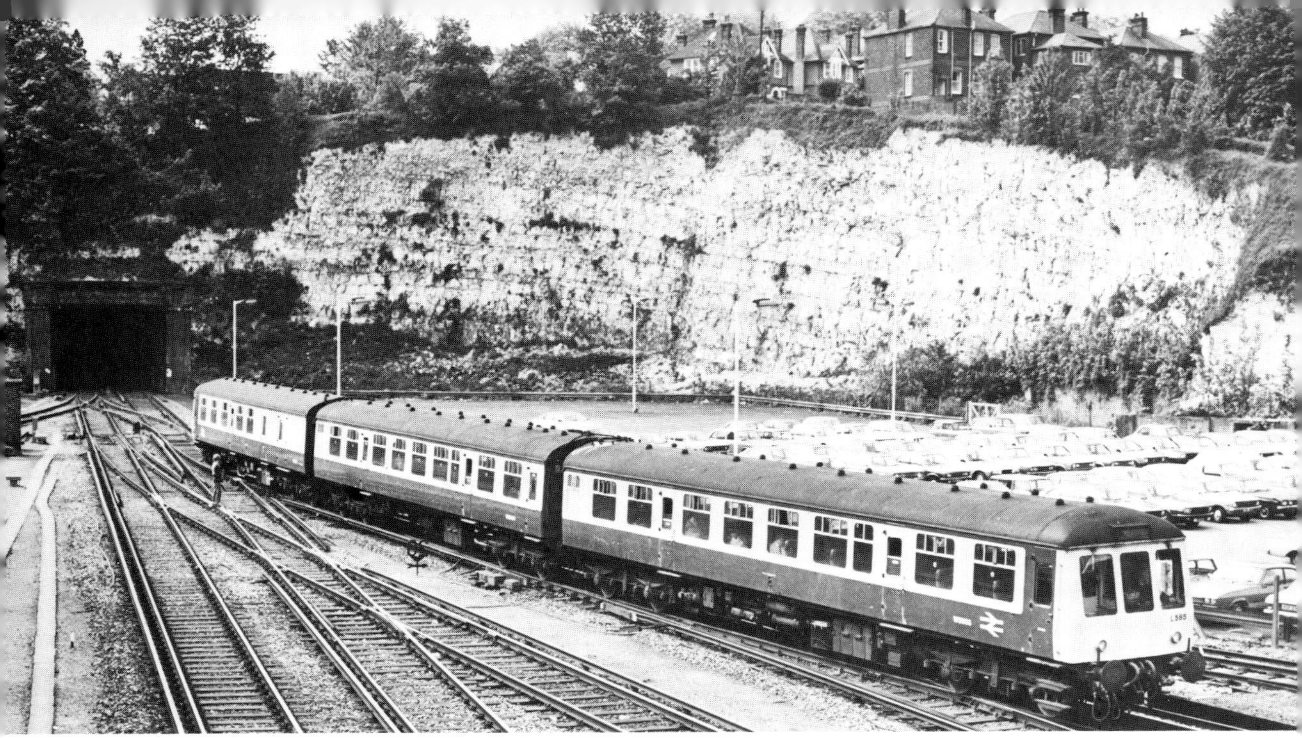

Above: An important cross-country connection for the SR is the Reading-Tonbridge line. This route was operated by SR demu stock until the beginning of the decade when WR dmu vehicles took over, thus improving the levels of passenger comfort. WR units used are usually of Class 119, allocated to Reading shed. Unit No L585 is seen here departing from Chalk Tunnel, Guildford, with a Tonbridge-Reading train on 13 May 1981. *John Faulkner*

Below: During 1980/81 a new cross-country connection was formed, based on the Reading-Tonbridge route, but with a fast service from Reading to Gatwick Airport, giving a rapid connection with WR stations to London's second airport. Trains take the same route as far as Redhill from where, after reversing, they take the CD Brighton main line to Gatwick. Having crossed from the Redhill lines to the down fast, unit No L577 approaches Earlswood on 20 April 1982. *John Faulkner*

Above: In the late afternoon there are several local services operated at the eastern end of the Reading-Tonbridge line, these are normally formed of SR Class 205 (3H) units. Running into Penshurst station No 1119 forms the 16.51 Tonbridge-Reigate on 27 July 1982. The train is carrying an incorrect headcode. *Michael Collins*

Left: The Ore-Portsmouth 'Coastway' line certainly falls into the category of a cross-country route, covering 86½ miles geographically east to west, although the line is separated into two distinct sections — 'East Coastway' from Ore-Brighton, and 'West Coastway' Brighton-Portsmouth. To improve passenger facilities on the route during 1982 24 Class 413 (4CAP) units were introduced by semi-permanently coupling together pairs of Class 414 (2HAP) units. Class 413 No 3307 approaches Havant with the 16.32 Brighton-Portsmouth on 12 June 1982. *Colin Marsden*

Above: During summer months the 'Coastway' line is well used with holiday passengers in addition to the regular passengers and there are also some daily commuters who use the line to connect with Havant for trains to Waterloo, or to Victoria from Brighton. Class 413 No 3201 stands at Barnham, the junction for the Bognor Regis line, with a Brighton-Portsmouth train on 7 June 1982. *Colin Marsden*

Below: Until the Brighton area signalling centre comes into operation during the latter part of the present decade, much of the semaphore signalling will remain in the area. Here at Hove are some interesting colour light signals mounted on home semaphore posts, controlled from the manual signalbox behind. Class 423 (4VEP) No 7806 approaches the station with a Brighton-Portsmouth stopping service. *John Vaughan*

Left: Departing from the western portals of Hastings tunnel a 2×Class 414 (2HAP) formation arrives at St Leonards Warrior Square station with an Ore-Brighton service. For the majority of the day the east 'Coastway' service is provided with two trains in each direction per hour, one semi-fast and the other slow. On the west section of the line a similar service operates. *John Vaughan*

Above: An interesting cross-country train which visits the CD every Saturday, is the through service to Exeter (Paignton on summer Saturdays during 1982). The train is usually hauled by a single Class 33 during winter months with a pair of Class 33s in the height of the summer season when the train is strengthened. However due to engineering work on 11 October 1980 the service was hauled by a Class 50 No 50.001 *Dreadnought.* The train is seen here at Brighton before departure. *John Vaughan*

Right: Passenger returns for the Brighton-Exeter (Paignton) line are favourable and the future of the service looks stable, but double-headed Class 33 motive power could well be replaced by a Class 47 in the foreseeable future. Class 33s Nos 33.104/010 haul the 13.40 Exeter-Brighton past Tisbury Gates on 2 May 1981. *John Vaughan*

Freight Traffic

Freight traffic on the Southern Region is mainly inter-regional or international and local movements are very limited.

The traditional coal traffic into the South of England now takes the form of MGR trains from the Nottinghamshire pits to the giant Northfleet cement works. These trains come on to the SR at Kew Bridge and for most of their journey to Northfleet have to run between frequent regular interval suburban electrics so that double heading with Class 45 or 47 locomotives was the rule until their replacement with Class 56 diesels during the early 1980s. In the opposite direction coal moves from the Kent collieries (Betteshanger and Tilmanstone) to Scunthorpe as well as to local industry on the Medway. Of the once extensive household coal traffic the residue is worked in block trains such as those from Acton Yard to coal concentration depots at Purley, Tolworth and Chessington.

Oil is now the predominant fuel and two major refineries are situated on the SR. Traffic from BP's Isle of Grain refinery is worked down the Hundred of Hoo branch to Hoo Junction where it is despatched to such destinations as Cardiff, Newbury, Thame and Kings Lynn, most trains being scheduled for Class 33 haulage. However the closure of this refinery threatens this traffic and the future of the branch beyond Cliffe.

The Esso refinery at Fawley distributes its products via the single line branch to Totton over an even wider area covering Plymouth, Tiverton Junction, Longport, Langley, Cambridge and Purfleet, and again Class 33 locomotives are in charge of most of these trains. Some oil traffic moves into the region, from Thames-side refineries via Ripple Lane yard to distribution depots at Micheldever and Earley often with Class 37 haulage throughout, and also to Gatwick Airport's oil sidings at Salfords, but this flow is soon to be replaced by pipeline transportation. A unique movement is the daily train of indigenous crude oil which leaves Furzebrook sidings on the Swanage branch for Llandarcy refinery in South Wales.

Cement is another major traffic and one of the largest works in the country is situated at Northfleet on the North Kent line, as well as various smaller works in the Medway Valley. Bulk cement in tank wagons is despatched from Northfleet to distribution depots at such points as Dunstable, Theale and Southampton. The counterpart to cement is stone and there is a regular flow of traffic from the Mendip quarries via Westbury and Salisbury to unloading points at Ardingly, Salfords, Hothfield, Eastleigh, Botley and Angerstein Wharf (Deptford), mostly worked by Class 47 locomotives. Another movement is from Cliffe on the Hoo branch to terminals at Purley, Stewarts Lane, Allington and King's Cross.

Freightliners Ltd has been most successful in securing maritime traffic and Southampton Docks is served by two freightliner terminals, at Millbrook and adjacent to the main container berths. Millbrook despatches trains to Lawley Street (Birmingham), Stratford, Coatbridge and Trafford Park (Manchester). Southampton Maritime Container Terminal (MCT) has departures for Leeds, Coatbridge, Aintree, Ripple Lane and Barton Dock Road (Manchester). All these trains are routed via Basingstoke and Reading, usually with Class 47 motive power but SR Class 33s are responsible for working to Coatbridge and Lawley Street, and while on Southern territory are often double headed.

International traffic arrives at Dover by train ferry and is forwarded by air braked Speedlink services to Willesden and Acton yards in London as well as more distant destinations served by Bescot and Tees yards. There is also a short distance shuttle between Dover and the Transfesa terminal at Paddock Wood conveying fruit and vegetables mainly from Spain.

Besides these major traffic flows there are various individual movements, often by Company trains; the Sheppey area generates several of these — outwards steel from the new Sheerness Steel works to the London marshalling yards and a through train from Ridham Dock to Tyne Yard, while inwards china clay arrives at Sittingbourne from Burngullow in Cornwall.

There is still some residual wagon load traditional traffic coming into the region by transfer workings from Acton or Temple Mills to Norwood Yard but the loose-coupled freight train and the brake van on the rear are no longer to be seen on SR. These transfer freights bring other regions' motive power on to the Southern, notable visitors being Class 31 and 37 locomotives, and in return SR engines work across London, including some lengthy penetrations of non-electrified tracks by the Class 73 electro-diesels.

The SR, often regarded as being a kind of commuter tramway, in fact carries quite a substantial share of the bulk and specialised traffics which form the core of BR's freight business in the 1980s.

Below: Just falling into the category of a freight train is the daily empty vans from Bournemouth and Eastleigh to Clapham Junction conveying stock off the southbound overnight newspaper services. Class 73 No 73.129 passes through New Malden station on 12 April 1980 carrying the legendary '02' headcode, meaning empties to Clapham Junction up passenger loop. *Colin Marsden*

Mail, Newspapers and Parcels

EMUs are not the only type of train running on the Southern electrified network. They cannot operate the nocturnal mail and newspaper trains formed of vans with two or three passenger coaches, which have to be hauled by diesel or electro-diesel locomotives. Examples are the 22.52 Waterloo-Weymouth, the traditional Dorchester mail, and the 23.40 London Bridge-Dover which still follows the original SER main line via Redhill with its Class 73 electro-diesel working on diesel power between Redhill and Tonbridge.

Newspaper trains depart from London termini between about two and four o'clock in the morning, not all of them carrying passengers, from Waterloo to Yeovil, Weymouth, Bournemouth and Portsmouth, from Victoria to Ramsgate and Dover and from London Bridge to Brighton, Hastings and Bexhill, but no longer from Holborn Viaduct right on Fleet Street's doorstep. The empty stock returns to London during the middle of the day. Rail parcels traffic is now much reduced but Redhill is still a major centre for Post Office business with a daily parcels train arriving from Manchester Mayfield via Guildford and connecting departures for Margate, Eastbourne and Brighton.

Below: Many freight trains can be observed at Clapham Junction hauled by a variety of motive power. Every Monday, Wednesday and Friday the 06.30 Westbury Angerstein Wharf aggregate train recesses at Clapham Junction during mid-morning for a crew change. The train is seen here at Clapham Junction Kensington siding headed by Class 47 No 47.285 on 11 August 1981. *Colin Marsden*

Bottom: Whilst operating over the four track sections of the Southern, freight traffic is usually confined to slow lines, but today many freights are permitted to operate at quite fast speeds. Class 47 No 47.178 hurries up the local line between Woking and West Byfleet with a stone train formed of 26 open mineral wagons on 8 March 1982. *Colin Marsden*

Above: Much freight traffic conveyed on SR is 'Railway Internal', this includes the movement of stone from the major quarries in Whatley, Tytherington and Meldon, on the WR. Class 33 No 33.022 arrives at Woking with a loaded train from Westbury consisting of Dogfish, Sealion and Mermaid type wagons. *Colin Marsden*

Below: Another of the 'Railway Internal' freight types is the spoil train, formed of Grampus, Medium, High Turbot, Dace or Tunny wagons. These wagons remove the old dirty ballast from the permanent way to one of the disposal points; on the SWD this is at Farnham. Class 33 No 33.003 passes Newnham with a Basingstoke-Woking empty spoil train on 15 April 1980. *Colin Marsden*

Above: There are two major freightliner terminals on the SWD of the SR, both located at Southampton. During the 1980s traffic from both the terminals has built up to around a dozen trains per day, travelling to London, the Midlands, the North East, North West and Scotland. Class 47 No 47.068 takes the Reading branch at Basingstoke with one of the daily northbound freightliners. *Andrew French*

Below: The air brake freight system has progressively grown during the 1980s with the SWD main line and the route to the docks at Dover being the main SR arteries for this type of traffic. Illustrated here Class 33/1 fitted with push-pull equipment approaches Winchester Junction with the 06.50 Willesden-Fratton via Eastleigh 'Speedlink' freight on 7 July 1981. *Colin Marsden*

Above: Although the speeds of freight trains has been gradually increased and many now travel up to 75mph, it is normal operating practice for freight traffic to be recessed and passenger trains to be given priority. Class 47 No 47.345 eases out of Bevois Park yard with an ABS freight from Furzebrook to Eastleigh during July 1981. *Colin Marsden*

Above left: Probably some of the most interesting trains to photograph today are freight trains, but alas the days of the unfitted freight have gone for ever on the SR and the region is now fully fitted, except for the movement of special loads or engineers' trains where special authority is given. A short fitted engineers' train headed by a Class 73 passes Ashtead in Surrey, heading for Norwood Yard. *John Vaughan*

Below left: Often engineers trains traverse routes where freight traffic is not normally seen. This was the case on 11 November 1981 when Class 33 No 33.020 was caught on film passing Effingham Junction with the 10.45 special from Raynes Park yard to Woking conveying concrete sections for bridge work. Effingham Junction on the New Guildford line is normally the host of an endless array of emu trains and rarely sees a locomotive, perhaps only once or twice a month. *Andrew French*

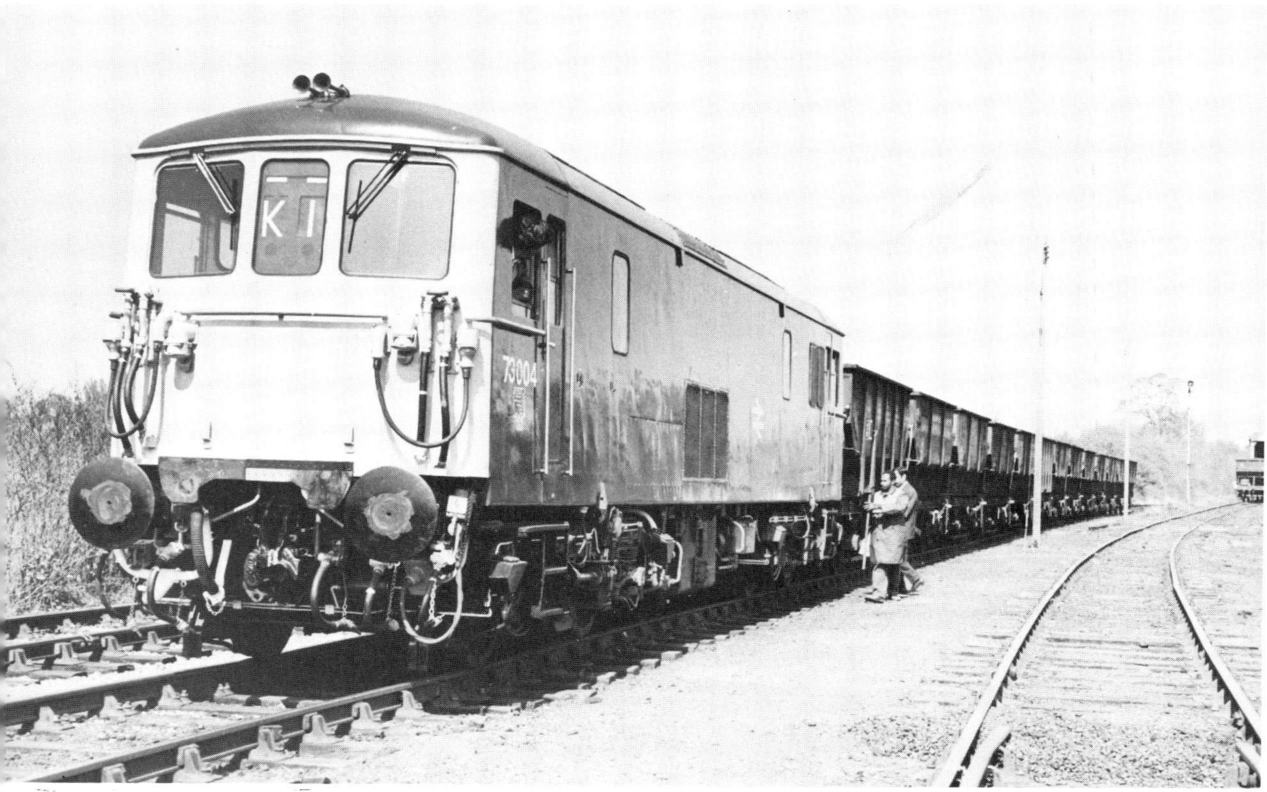
K I
73004

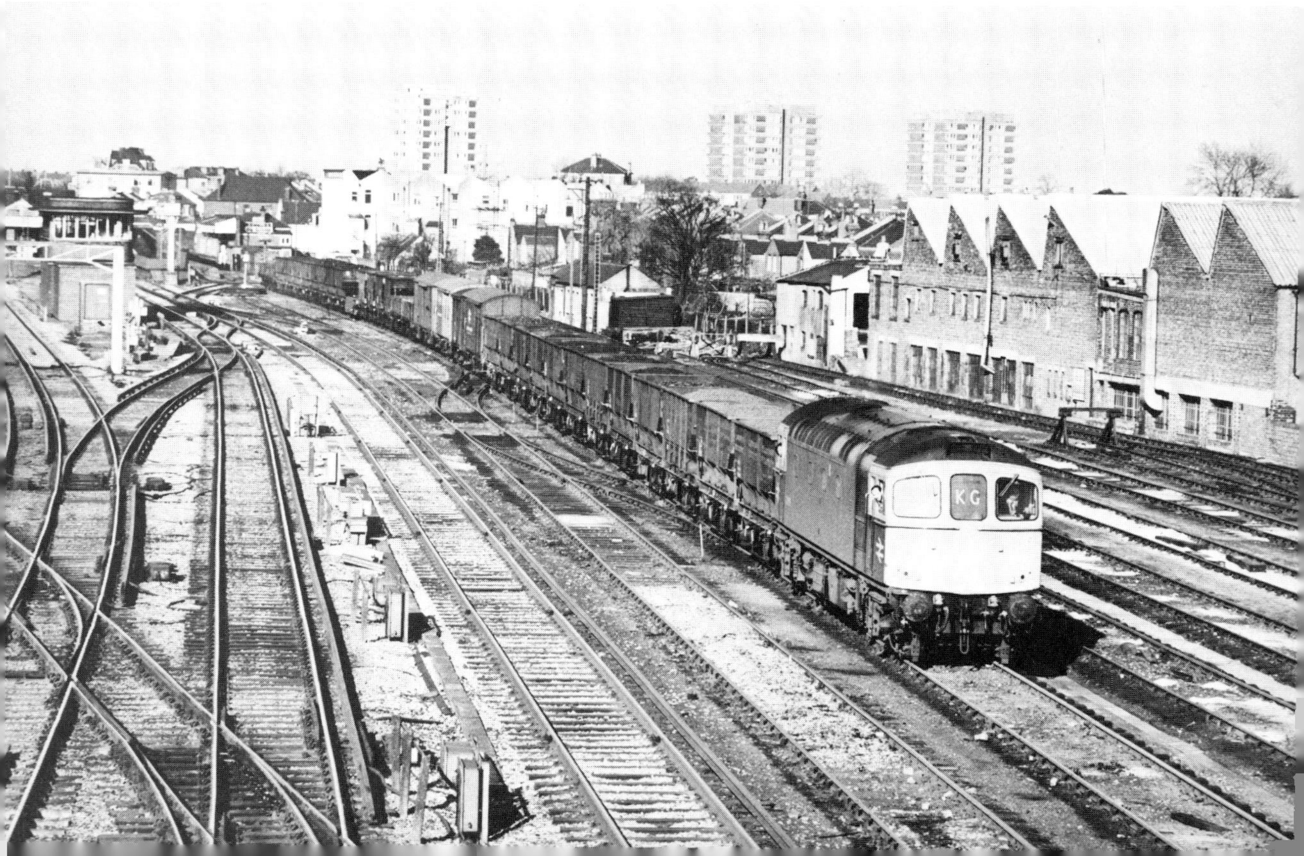
KG

Above left: For many years the suburban SWD line to Chessington has seen coal traffic to two rail heads on the branch, one at Tolworth and the other at Chessington South. One of the six prototype Class 73s No 73.004 stands in the coal yard at Chessington after arrival from South Wales via Acton and Wimbledon, however the Class 73 would have only worked the train from Acton. *Colin Marsden*

Left: The largest concentration of freight on the CD for many years has been at Norwood Junction, however the major marshalling yards closed here during the early 1980s following the general decline in rail borne freight traffic. Class 33 No 33.055 arrives in one of the reception lines at Norwood Junction with the 13.15 Acton-New Cross Gate freight on 5 March 1982. *Colin Marsden*

Above: During the early 1980s a thrice weekly oil tank train from Fratton supplied the Cory distribution terminal at Portfield, east of Chichester on the coastway line. Motive power for these trains although diagrammed for an electro-diesel, is often provided by Class 33 locomotives. On 13 May 1981 Class 33 No 33.034 arrives at the junction points for the terminal line. *Les Bertram*

Right: The cross-country line between Tonbridge-Redhill-Guildford and Reading sees a large amount of freight movements, as this line provides a suitable connection between the three divisions. Hastings profile Class 33/2 No 33.201 passes near the village of Crowhurst on the non-electrified route with the 11.00 Tonbridge West Yard-Norwood freight. *Brian Denton*

Left: Another advance during the late 1970s and early 1980s has been the wider use of block load trains, a regular sight on the SR are the powdered cement trains working to and from Halling, Holbrough, Northfleet and Northam. Passing through London suburbs and approaching Longhedge Junction Class 33 No 33.045 hauls a cement train formed of high capacity bogie hoppers bound for the ER on 24 September 1980. *Colin Marsden*

Below far left: A departmental special freight from Ashford to Hither Green permanent way yard headed by Class 73 No 73.133 passes Five Oak Green on 4 June 1982. The train is conveying concrete sleepers and cable troughing not used on weekend engineering work. Trains such as this are fitted with vacuum brakes only, and before the decade is out it is likely that the majority of vehicles will have been withdrawn and replaced by modern purpose built air brake fitted vehicles. *Colin Marsden*

Below: Vans that operate overnight from London to the East Kent towns are worked back to the London area during the day and stabled at New Cross Gate. Class 73 No 73.134 running under its electric conditions hauls a mixture of bogie and four-wheeled vans between Ashford and Pluckley on 15 May 1980. *Colin Marsden*

Below: Much of the imported and exported fruit and perishables use the docks at Dover thus giving sufficient demand for the provision of several trains each day. One of the main storage and distribution areas for fruit is at Paddock Wood. This terminal is provided with a service from and to Dover each weekday morning, and the train headed by Class 33 No 33.047 was photographed soon after leaving the Terminal and heading back to Dover on 4 June 1982. *Colin Marsden*

Bottom: Each afternoon ABS freights conveying perishables depart from Dover bound for Bescot and Tees Yard. The train to Bescot is routed via Canterbury whereas the Tees Yard service travels via Ashford. Departing from Sandling Tunnel Class 33 No 33.053 hauls the 16.18 Dover-Tees Yard on 2 June 1982. The train is conveying an interesting collection of British and Continental vehicles. *Colin Marsden*

Above: A Mondays excepted oil train runs from Hoo Junction to Brookgate, situated between Aylesford and New Hythe. This train is usually hauled by a Class 73 electro-diesel and works to Maidstone West where the locomotive runs round the train. Following this move Class 73 No 73.114 pulls through the station and regains the down line on 3 June 1982. *Colin Marsden*

Below: A daily jaunt for a SR locomotive and crew is to Thame on the former Oxford-Princes Risborough branch. On SR the train operates from and to Hoo Junction. Fitted with two miniature snowploughs Class 33 No 33.049 hauls the 09.40 Thame-Hoo Junction past Northfleet on 29 May 1981. *Colin Marsden*

Locomotive & Stock Maintenance

With the SR operating some 5,134 trains each day the regular maintenance of the Region's fleets of 1,161 emu, 74 dmu and 190 locomotives (94 main line diesel-electric, 47 electro-diesel, 47 diesel shunting, and two departmental) is of prime importance, as more than 85% of the fleets have to be in operation each day to ensure a full public service. Locomotive maintenance apart from 'in service' repairs, is usually carried out at one of the larger locomotive depots ie Eastleigh, Hither Green, Stewarts Lane, Ashford or Selhurst. The backbone motive power for the Southern, the Class 33s, are allocated between Eastleigh and Hither Green, with both depots being equipped to undertake programmed maintenance, major repairs, including minor collision damage, and have the facility to lift locomotives clear of their bogies, for bogie, wheel, and underframe attention. Every 3-4 years each locomotive is admitted, by programmed maintenance, to the SR's main BREL works at Eastleigh for classified repairs involving the stripping down of all components and rebuilding the locomotive from its bare carcass. Unlike the procedure on other Regions, it is unusual for Eastleigh Works to undertake any collision damage repairs and these are usually dealt with at Slade Green. Fuelling and service checks of Class 33s can be undertaken at various points around the Region, and it is not uncommon for St Leonards depot at Hastings, and Stewarts Lane depot in London, to undertake repairs, depending on workloads at the various depots.

The Southern's unique fleet of Class 73 electro-diesel locomotives are all allocated to Stewarts Lane depot, near Battersea, from where the fleet operate and are maintained, only receiving 'in service' maintenance at other depots. A unique feature of the Class 73 allocation is that although Stewarts Lane is a South Eastern Division Depot, all three of the Southern's divisions are served. The electric shed at Stewarts Lane was purpose built in the late 1950s for the Kent Coast electrification and is fully equipped to undertake all necessary repairs to the class, however bogie repairs are usually carried out at Selhurst, and major collision repairs at Slade Green.

The Region's allocation of Class 08 and 09 350hp diesel-electric shunting locomotives is divided between Eastleigh, Selhurst and Ashford, with each depot providing shunting power for a wide area. Due to the nature of the shunting locomotive's work it is not necessary (except for fuel) for the locomotive to return to its home depot for several weeks, and even in areas such as Clapham Junction, where shunting duties are carried out round the clock, the same locomotive is used for up to three weeks at a time.

Each day many foreign allocated locomotives of various classes visit the SR, usually on an 'in-out' basis, but the SWD does operate several WR Class 50 locomotives on its Waterloo-Exeter service. These are provided by Laira shed in Plymouth and should not require maintenance on the SR except fuel and water. However, the maintenance schedules of the WR are perhaps not as good as what they should be, and often their locomotives have to be maintained by Eastleigh or Stewarts Lane. Class 47s are frequently given service checks and exams by Eastleigh when operating inter-regional passenger or freight services and sometimes remain on the region for several days, but of course any major faults would be referred to the locomotive's home depot.

The Region's DEMU fleet is allocated to Eastleigh and St Leonards from where all duties are based; Eastleigh allocated units operating on the Portsmouth-Salisbury, Eastleigh-Portsmouth, and Reading-Salisbury services, while St Leonards units operate on the Central and South Eastern Divisions.

Again all scheduled and routine maintenance is carried out at the unit's home depot, but fuelling and service checks may be performed where the unit is operating. On the Reading-Tonbridge, and Reading-Gatwick lines WR allocated DMU stock is used, these are fully maintained by their owning region, and apart from very minor repairs, cannot be maintained by the SR.

The Southern's main passenger power is the EMU. These are allocated to all three divisions and each depot is fully equipped to undertake all necessary repairs and maintenance, apart from the main works at Eastleigh which undertakes all major classified repairs on a programmed basis. The SR has its own small workshops at Selhurst, Slade Green and Chart Leacon. These depots can carry out repaints, general overhauls (electrical) and other reasonably major overhauls — units visit these CM&EE maintenance depots at least once between each major works overhaul. Due to the size and complexity of operations it is not possible for each unit to visit its home depot each day and therefore units may receive maintenance at a shed to which it is not allocated. Although technical maintenance cannot be carried out there are a number of carriage stabling sidings throughout the Region where coach sweeping and cleaning is undertaken. Perhaps the

general public would not agree by the appearance of most units but at the larger depots automatic coach washing machines are provided where each unit arriving on depot passes through. Each unit scheduled maintenance includes an acid body wash which is carried out by the automatic washing machines.

The Region's fleet of loco-hauled stock, and visiting stock from inter-regional services, is usually maintained at Bournemouth, Eastleigh, Clapham Junction, New Cross Gate or Brighton, major repairs being undertaken by Carriage & Wagon (C&W) depots at Clapham Junction and Selhurst, and programmed classified overhauls at Eastleigh BREL works.

The parcel fleets are usually maintained by the above carriage depots, but as the majority of vehicles stray far and wide, various depots will undertake repairs, and except for a few non-passenger carrying coaching stock (NPCCS) vehicles, vans and parcel vehicles are not solely used by the SR.

Below: Two depots are responsible for the maintenance of the Region's Class 33 fleet, Eastleigh and Hither Green. At the end of 1982 Eastleigh were responsible for 52 locomotives, while Hither Green had 42 locomotives on its books. Parked inside the running shed at Hither Green on 23 November 1981 stands slim line Class 33/2 No 33.206. All slim bodied Class 33s are allocated to HG. *Ian Gould*

Above: Eastleigh diesel depot, in Hampshire, supplies all Class 33 locomotives for the SWD. The depot is fully equipped to undertake all repairs, and adjoining the running shed is a substantial CM&EE maintenance section, where extended maintenance can be undertaken. With a 'Not to be moved' board firmly on the front lamp iron Class 33 No 33.013 stands inside the running shed on 17 October 1981. *Colin Marsden*

Left: The 47 Class 73 electro-diesel locomotives are all allocated to Stewarts Lane depot in London, and although this depot is under the control of the CD it supplies all three divisions with these dual power machines. The depot was purpose built to deal with electric locomotives in the late 1950s and is fully equipped to undertake any maintenance necessary. No 73.142 *Broadlands* is seen here emerging from the shed in resplendent condition just prior to its naming ceremony. *Colin Marsden*

Right: Apart from depots where locomotives are allocated the region has a number of stabling points that have maintenance staff on hand to carry out necessary service checks. Brighton has a sizeable emu train shed and maintenance building with a small locomotive stabling point adjoining, shown here containing Class 73 No 73.138 and Class 33s Nos 33.019/059. *Colin Marsden*

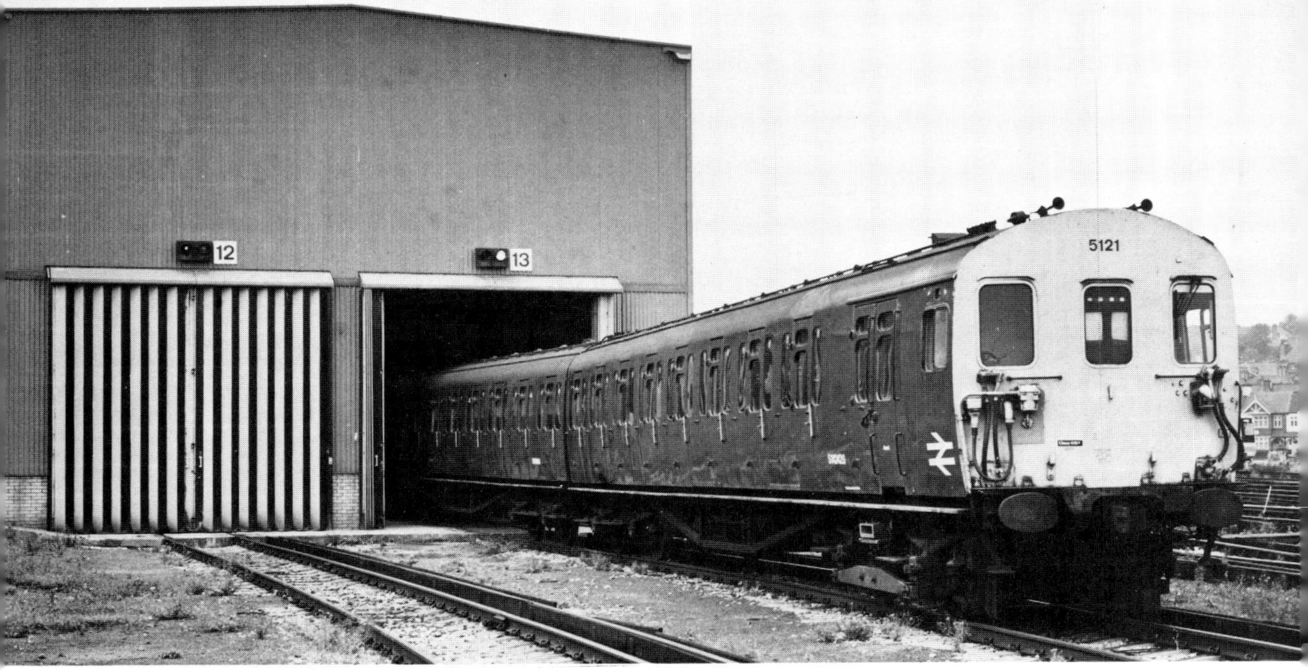
12
13
5121

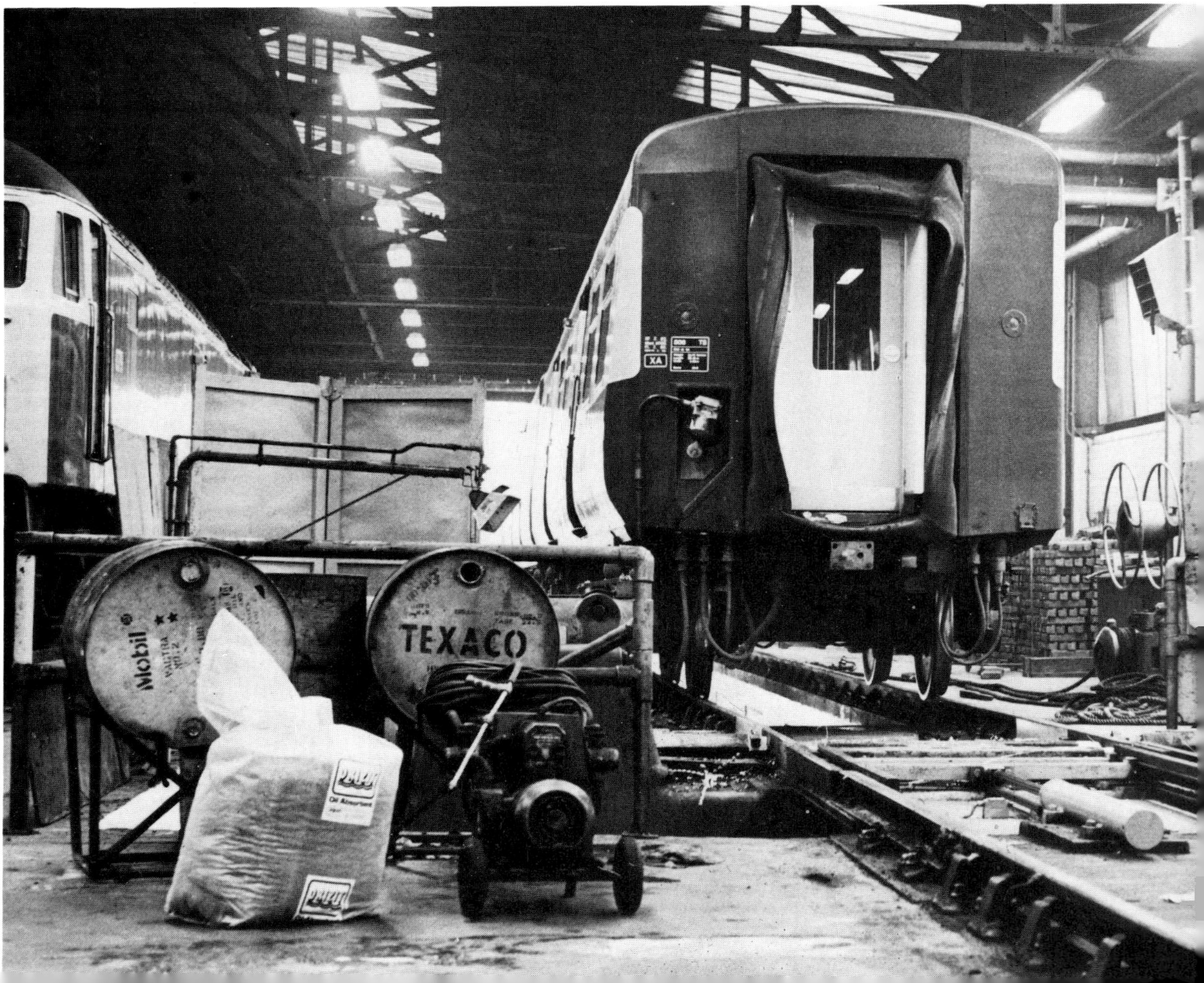
Mobil
TEXACO

Above far left: Substantial emu sheds and depots can be found all over the SR. At Wimbledon, $7\frac{1}{4}$ miles from Waterloo lays one of the largest depots with a current allocation of 646 coaches made up into 185 units. A purpose built maintenance shed was built during the mid-1970s to cater for the operating requirements of the 1980s. Parked partly inside the heavy maintenance shed Class 415 (4EPB) No 5121 receives electrical repairs on 14 October 1981. *Colin Marsden*

Left: Although Class 508 units are all allocated to East Wimbledon depot and operate only on the SWD suburban lines, maintenance is often carried out at other depots. If wheels have to be ground down to the correct profile the wheel lathe at Eastleigh is often used. A TS vehicle from a Class 508 is pictured parked just clear of the lathe on 17 October 1981. *Colin Marsden*

Above: Apart from Eastleigh Works which undertakes all classified and major overhauls on the Region's emu stock, there is a heavy maintenance shop at Slade Green. Here anything from minor component changes to collision repairs are undertaken. Receiving bogie attention Class 508 No 508.022 stands inside Slade Green repair shop on 6 February 1982. *John Faulkner*

Left: Some daily passengers may find it hard to believe that the SR do wash the outside of their trains. Each major depot and some of the smaller ones are fitted with carriage washing machines. Here the one at Selhurst cleans Class 415 (4EPB) No 5415. An endeavour is made to wash as many units each day as is practical.   *Colin Marsden*

Above: At Clapham Junction in the junction between the main and the Windsor lines of the SWD, there is a considerable stabling point for emu, locomotives and locomotive hauled stock, with over 50 sidings with a capacity to hold more than 450 vehicles at any one time. During the day part of the yard is used to stable emus awaiting their return trips south with the evening peak services. Parked protruding from the servicing shed on 24 January 1981 is Class 421 (4CIG) No 7338. *Colin Marsden*

Right: Throughout the early years of the decade a major refurbishing programme has been undertaken on the Kent Coast Class 411 units to bring them into line with the requirements of the 1980s. Coaches are taken to Swindon works for attention being locomotive hauled to and from the SR by Class 33 or 73 locomotives. Strawberry Hill is used for testing the units on return from refurbishment and it is here that unit No 411.608 stands at the beginning of 1980. *Colin Marsden*

Behind the Scenes

On the Southern Region, like all regions of the British Rail network, there are many activities undertaken that the public are little or unaware of. Most of these activities could be classed under the heading of departmental train operations, but at times and in some locations, trains and equipment not in the departmental fleet are used and therefore illustrated here.

One activity in which most weekend passengers have been involved at some time, is engineering work. This can include many different operations such as relaying track or points, rebuilding lineside structures, bridges or tunnels, or general maintenance work. In most cases the presence of trains in the area of work would be a hindrance and likely to prolong delays. Usually when essential work has to be undertaken a section of line, or complete branch line, is taken out of use and placed under the possession of the relevant engineering department, with the only trains allowed into the section being those engaged on the work in progress. For the period of line occupation, normally referred to by railwaymen as 'the block', passenger and other services are either diverted around the obstruction, or terminated short with connecting bus services provided. Normally this kind of work can be confined to weekends, usually a Sunday, but occasionally where large jobs have to be undertaken, evening and night possession may become essential. During the early part of the 1980s the Central Division probably underwent the most extensive engineering work, with major resignalling schemes undertaken at Victoria and Clapham Junction, involving the majority of the Division's suburban lines. Much track rationalisation has also taken place especially on the main Brighton line, where in places such as between Selhurst and East Croydon, the old layout is now hardly recognisable. On the Eastern and Western sections much routine maintenance has

continued to take place and much has centred on track rationalisation and modernising the signalling systems, and replacing old fashioned semaphore signals with the latest computer based electronic equipment. By the end of this decade it is unlikely that any semaphore signalling equipment will remain in use on the SR and in all probability several of the earlier built panel boxes will be replaced by larger area signalling centres. The trains that normally operate with engineering work are classified as departmental trains and exclusively convey departmental rolling stock. When not in use they can be seen at one of the Region's civil engineering yards at Woking, Three Bridges, New Cross Gate, Hither Green, Eastleigh or Ashford (Kent), each of which has an allocation of cranes and associated track equipment. The new track itself is formed and pre-assembled at the Region's civil engineering track section at Redbridge, near Southampton. After any track maintenance has been carried out, and also at periodic intervals, a tamper, liner or ballast machine operates over the tracks gauging, lining and packing where necessary, a job formerly done by hand. From time to time the rail grinding (SPENO) train visits the Region, this seven-coach departmental train is fitted with grinding wheels to reprofile the tracks.

Items of essential railway equipment normally kept behind the scenes are the breakdown cranes and their associated vans, and the SR operates quite a sizeable fleet of these vehicle considering the mileage of its system. Cranes and rerailing vehicles are allocated to Wimbledon Park, Eastleigh, Stewarts Lane, Brighton, Hither Green and Ashford (Kent) depots. The two cranes allocated to the SWD are both of the 75ton diesel hydraulic type, while those of the other Divisions are generally equipped only to lift loads up to 45ton. Each crane has its own allocated area to cover in case of derailment, but if a major incident occurs often two or more cranes will attend depending on the location and seriousness of the accident. In addition to using cranes to rerail vehicles, a fleet of road mobile hydraulic-operated jacks can be used, these being suitable to rerail a complete locomotive if it has come to rest in the upright position and is near to the rails. Occasionally these cranes are used for weekend engineering work where their bigger lifting capability may be an asset in bridge or structural rebuilding work.

Although 99% of the Region's emus are far from being classified as behind the scenes, several former passenger carrying units have found further use. With the SR electrification being of the third rail type, snow and ice soon form on the rails and electric pickup surface, causing loss of power collection. To ease this problem a fleet of de-icing trains operate, formed of two motor-coaches from former HAL and SUB stock, fitted with third rail scraping equipment and de-icing fluid layers. When inclement and below freezing temperatures are forecast, units operate from strategic depots covering all routes of the system in an endeavour to operate a trouble-free service. The Region also has three trailer de-icing vans, these are former suburban unit trailer cars fitted with scraping and fluid laying equipment and able to operate between conventional passenger carrying emu stock. For staff training purposes a withdrawn 4SUB unit was converted during 1974 to act as a mobile classroom for CM&EE department staff. Although the vehicle saw much use when new, so far during the 1980s it has remained either at East Wimbledon or Chart Leacon depots and cannot have justified the cost of its conversion. With many thousands of emu formed trains operating daily on SR, the maintenance of the equipment must take prime place and a ready supply of spare parts at the depot is of supreme importance. To ensure this continuity a fleet of three two-car sets operate as stores units between Eastleigh works, Slade Green and Chart Leacon to all the region's maintenance points, with items ranging from major brake equipment to the smallest screws. The three units each have a set diagram which covers all points on the maintenance circuit at least once a week.

At Strawberry Hill, on the Kingston roundabout line, the CM&EE department have a substantial Rolling Stock Development section (RSD) which during the 1980s has been building up and now have purpose built accommodation housing various items of sophisticated equipment. Operating from this centre are a small fleet of test vehicles and units, mainly for traction equipment development. Another use for the centre came during the early 1980s to test the new Class 508 emu units as they were delivered from the BREL works at York, testing normally taking place between Strawberry Hill and Shepperton. When the delivery of Class 455 units commenced at the end of 1982 again Strawberry Hill played a large part in their commission and testing.

When it was realised that the SR would not be receiving large numbers of 'new units' for a considerable period of time, it was decided to commence a refurbishment programme on selected classes. The first class to be modernised was the Kent coast electrification 4BEP/CEP (Class 410/411) main line units built between 1956 and 1963 which did not now provide the standard of interior comfort required on a main line unit. Unit No 7153 was refurbished at Eastleigh and then evaluated. Upon successful completion a contract was given to British Railway Engineering Limited (BREL) to undertake the full refurbishment of the class. As their works at Eastleigh were doubtful about meeting the required delivery deadlines, Swindon works were awarded the contract necessitating all stock passing through the works being hauled by a locomotive to and from the Southern. Other problems now arose such as unit testing, which could not be fully carried out at Swindon where no third-rail connection was available, only a shore supply, and this proved inadequate for thorough testing. During the years of the refurbishing scheme it has been established practice for units to operate from the SED where they are allocated to Strawberry Hill, under their own power. After removal of some electrical equipment and shoe beams the units continued on to Swindon works reception sidings usually hauled by a Class 33/1 or 73/1 locomotive, utilising their high-level air pipes for a through train brake connection. On the return journey sets were hauled to Strawberry Hill where full testing could be carried out, including trial running on the Shepperton branch, this often in company with test car DB975032 *Mars*. Normally units were out of traffic for some 4-5 months during their refurbishment.

Another unit modernisation scheme commenced during the early 1980s when members of the Class 415 (4EPB) fleet started to receive 'facelift' overhauls incorporating the replacement and updating of interiors, fitting lower ceilings, fluorescent lighting and a public address system. This programme was divided between Eastleigh and Horwich works. The units dealt with at Eastleigh were easily operated to and from the works under their own power and testing could be carried out in the works, but with the Class 410/411 units being repaired at Swindon causing distance problems, the Class 415s undergoing modernisation at Horwich also experienced similar difficulties having to be hauled some 195 miles to and from their repair point. With little testing equipment available at Horwich units had to undergo testing on their return to the SR, and in more than one case a unit had to return to Horwich for adjustments.

During 1982/3 further facelift programmes commenced to bring units in to line with modern requirements. In 1982 a start was made on the 2EPB (Class 416) fleet and by the turn of the year some of the BR-built 4EPB (Class 415/2) units were undergoing facelifts at Eastleigh works. After the present Class 410/411 programme is completed it is expected that it will be the turn of 1963 built 4BIG/CIG (Class 420/421s), but with present uncertainty with regard to the future of BREL Swindon these repairs may well be undertaken at Eastleigh or some other works.

All drivers and guards need to be fully acquainted with the routes they are required to work over and this experience is usually gained by riding with another driver or guard who is fully conversant with the route, but where trains are few or far between or where route knowledge is required quickly, special 'route learning' trains are operated. Sometimes these are formed of emu or dmu stock but more often if crews are Southern men one of two special route learning observation cars will be used, being either hauled or propelled by a diesel or electro-diesel locomotive. Each route learning programme lasts for five days and consists of between 8-12 men, instruction being given by a Motive Power Inspector.

The average member of the travelling public does not cast a second glance at the locomotives that have been named during the 1980s to honour or signify special occasions. Two Class 33s, Nos 33.027/056 which hauled the funeral train of Earl Mountbatten of Burma from Waterloo to Romsey on 5 September

Below: For depot shunting at Slade Green Class 08 No 08.600 was taken into departmental use following withdrawal and numbered 97.800 and named *Ivor*. During 1981 the locomotive visited Selhurst shops for an overhaul and emerged painted in departmental red/blue livery. No 97.800 stands outside Slade Green depot in this May 1981 photograph. *Colin Marsden*

1979 were named *Earl Mountbatten of Burma* and *Burma Star* respectively at Waterloo during the summer of 1980 by members of the Mountbatten family. Two other Class 33s, Nos 33.008/052 were named *Eastleigh* and *Ashford* during 1980 in acknowledgment of each town's long association with the railway industry. In 1981 Class 33 No 33.025 received the name *Sultan* in recognition of the Naval Training Establishment. Three of the Region's Class 73 electro-diesel locomotives have also been named. In September 1980 No 73.142 was named *Broadlands* after the home of the late Lord Mountbatten of Burma, this engine chosen because it hauled the empty stock between Clapham Junction and Waterloo on the day of the Earl's funeral. The second Class 73, No 73.101 (renumbered 73.100 for the ceremony) became *Brighton Evening Argus* to commemorate the centenary of the evening paper of that name, and during December 1982 No 73.129 was named *City of Winchester*.

Two significant railway events kept 'behind the scenes' until the day were the Prince & Princess of Wales' Royal Wedding train from Waterloo to Romsey on 29 July 1981, and the train which transported Pope John Paul II between Gatwick Airport and Victoria in May 1982. For both of these events Class 73 No 73.142 *Broadlands* powered

standard loco-hauled coaches and the SR General Manager's Saloon No DB975025 at the rear. Tight security surrounded these trains and prior to their working were locked-up overnight at Stewarts Lane depot.

The SR is occasionally host to some of Britain's most unwelcome trains — those conveying nuclear waste. Vehicles used for this purpose are formed into special trains and usually operate at night, often visiting the South Esatern Division and very occasionally the South Western section. Such is the security surrounding these trains that members of the public are discouraged from showing any interest in them and if cameras are seen pointing in their direction action is likely to be taken. However, with London becoming a nuclear free zone during 1982 the operation of these trains became very restricted.

Below: When the Waterloo & City rolling stock requires maintenance, usually carried out at Selhurst, the cars have to be brought to the surface via the Armstrong hydraulic lift, situated in the north sidings of Waterloo station. From here the vehicles are marshalled between match wagons and hauled as an unfitted load. Class 73 No 73.003 prepares to depart from Waterloo bound for Selhurst on 20 August 1981 hauling Class 487 car No S56. *Colin Marsden*

Above: Being propelled down the up line at Haslemere is the SR route learning saloon No TDB 395280. The coach which was formerly the Watford District Engineer's saloon was transferred to the SR during early 1970 to assist with driver and guard route training. Normally up to 12 drivers and guards are given tuition by a motive power inspector. When this photograph was taken on 19 February 1981 motive power was provided by Class 33 No 33.026.
Andrew French

Below: Each weekend part of the region is placed under the possession of the CCE staff for the purpose of track relaying or replacing old pointwork. Class 73 No 73.138 stands in the up main platform line at Surbiton on 11 October 1981 whilst supplying equipment for the relaying of the down main line, slightly further south. Often trains such as this can bring an archaic collection of wagons and make interesting photography. *Colin Marsden*

Top: During the autumn of 1981 the Swiss company of Speno loaned BR their vehicle SM775 which is for rail surface measuring. With a driving position at both ends the car is seen here at Stewarts Lane depot after completing a trip on the SED. *Colin Marsden*

Above: At Strawberry Hill, near Twickenham, in the triangle of lines between Strawberry Hill, Fulwell and Teddington stations there is an emu depot with an adjoining Rolling Stock Development (RSD) section. This Section undertakes tests on new stock as well as commissioning the refurbished Class 411 units on their return from Swindon. For a period during early 1980s much withdrawn emu stock was parked at the depot and very little used. This was the fate of Class 414 (2HAP) No 6127 after being withdrawn following collision damage the unit spent 18 months at Strawberry Hill before being sold for scrap during 1982. *Colin Marsden*

Right: The eldest of the emu trains in operation during the early 1980s were the stores and de-icing units, some of which date back to the late 1930s. Stores units have all their internal seating removed and have a large sliding door for the ease of loading. Unit No 022 is seen here at Stewarts Lane electric depot on 26 March 1980, this unit was withdrawn at the end of 1982. *Colin Marsden*

Below: De-icing units are used in adverse weather conditions scrapeing and laying de-icing fluid on the third-rail to stop freezing up. The same units are also used as rail cleaners during the autumn by spraying a mixture of sand and glue on to the rails to prevent units from slipping. Set No 001 passes Wimbledon West while heading for Effingham Junction on 17 October 1981. *Colin Marsden*

Top: In extreme bad weather it is possible for even the de-icing units to become stuck in the snow, when a diesel or electro-diesel locomotive is attached to give assistance. The de-icing units are fitted with multiple unit control equipment to enable them to operate with electro-diesel or push-pull fitted Class 33/1s. Unit No 009 is photographed here on the outskirts of Bournemouth in company with a Class 73 No 73.119 on 11 January 1982. *Michael Ricks*

Above: Throughout the 1970s the prototype high-density PEP unit operated various trials on SR. At the end of the decade it returned to Derby where further test equipment was fitted and on its return to SR was painted in experimental livery similar to that applied to the APT. During 1980 the units operated various bogie tests on SWD main lines but during 1981/2 saw little or no work. Carrying No 4002 the unit is seen dumped at East Wimbledon depot during April 1981. *Colin Marsden*

Above: On an approximate 12 month's cycle the BRB track testing coach No DB999550 visits most of the major lines in the country, with lesser used lines on a longer cycle. On 8 August 1980 it was the turn of the Mid-Sussex line to be inspected and the coach is seen here between two locomotive hauled coaches with Class 33 No 33.015 at the head, near Horsham. *John Vaughan*

Below: When the test car visits some areas it is accompanied by interesting motive power. This was the case on 15 December 1981 when the vehicle was diagrammed to test the BR lines between Wimbledon and the BR/LT boundary at Putney Bridge. Although the line is electrified it would not have been practical to use emus with the car, so two spare Class 201 (6S) DBSOs were used. Here standing in platform 4 at Wimbledon the two Class 201 cars with the test car between them await departure. *Colin Marsden*

Left: On 16 July 1981 three London Transport vehicles operated over the BR network. The train formed of a pilot motor car at each end and LT's rail grinder between operated trial runs on the Kingston-Shepperton line, and is seen here in the bay platform at Kingston with pilot motor No L131 nearest the camera. *Colin Marsden*

Below left: The SR like the other regions have had pleasure in naming some of their locomotives during the last few years. On 3 December 1980 to mark the 100th anniversary of the newspaper *Brighton Evening Argus*, Class 73/1 No 73.101 (temporarily renumbered 73.100 for the event) was named at Brighton Station by the Editor and his wife *Brighton Evening Argus*. The locomotive is seen here before the ceremony. *Colin Marsden*

Right: On 6 August 1981 Class 33 No 33.025 was twinned with the Naval Shore establishment HMS *Sultan* and given the name in a special ceremony held at Portsmouth Harbour station. In the picture Captain Austin Lockyer unveils the plate with the superb coat-of-arms beneath. It is hoped that further Class 33 namings will take place in the future. *Colin Marsden*

Below right: Following the death of Earl Mountbatten of Burma during 1979, and the SR providing the motive power for the funeral train from Waterloo to Romsey, the three locomotives involved were all named. The two Class 33s that hauled the train Nos 33.027/056 received the names *Earl Mountbatten of Burma*, and *Burma Star* respectively. The engine that hauled the empty stock into Waterloo No 73.142 was named *Broadlands* at Romsey station on 25 September 1980. In this picture Mr Neil (Divisional Motive Power Officer), Mr Ing (Regional Motive Power Officer), Mr Jupp (CM&EE Dept Southern House), Mr Stoneman (Driver's assistant of the empty funeral train), Mr Stevens (SW Divisional Motive Power Inspector), Mr Parsons (CM&EE Stewarts Lane) and Mr Boyce (Driver of the empty funeral train) stand by the side of the newly named locomotive. *Colin Marsden*

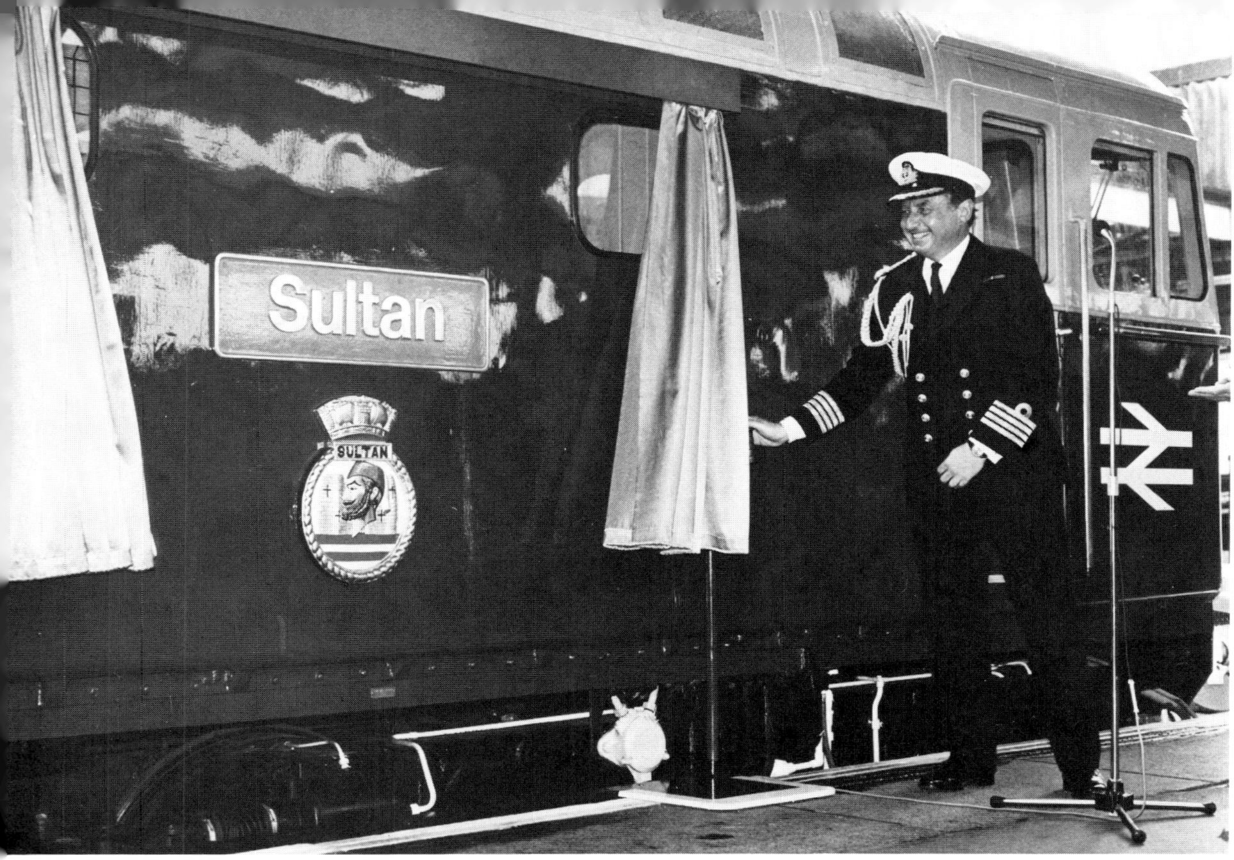
Sultan
SULTAN

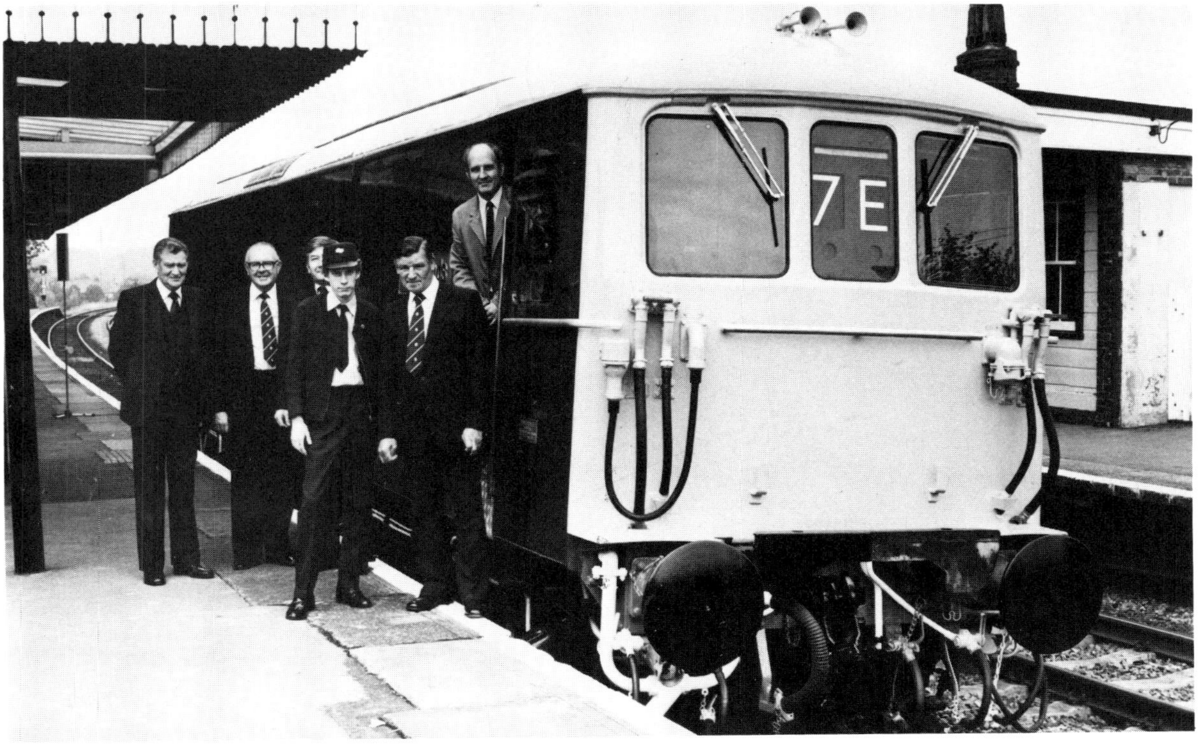
7E

Above: Following the wedding of the Prince and Princess of Wales on 29 July 1981, BR provided a special Royal Train from Waterloo to Romsey for the first stage of their honeymoon at Broadlands. The train was formed just of three cars with the SR General Manager's saloon on the rear, seen here headed by Class 73 No 73.142 *Broadlands* approaching Surbiton. The resplendent turn out of the locomotive and stock was the workmanship of the depot staff at Stewarts Lane. *Colin Marsden*

Below: When Pope John Paul II came on his historic visit to Britain during 1982 a special train conveyed him from Gatwick Airport to Victoria. The SR General Manager's saloon was again used for this occasion, together with two FO and one BCK coach. To ensure a smooth ride on the day, a test train was organised on 20 April and is seen here headed by Class 73 No 73.142 *Broadlands* passing Earlswood. *Colin Marsden*

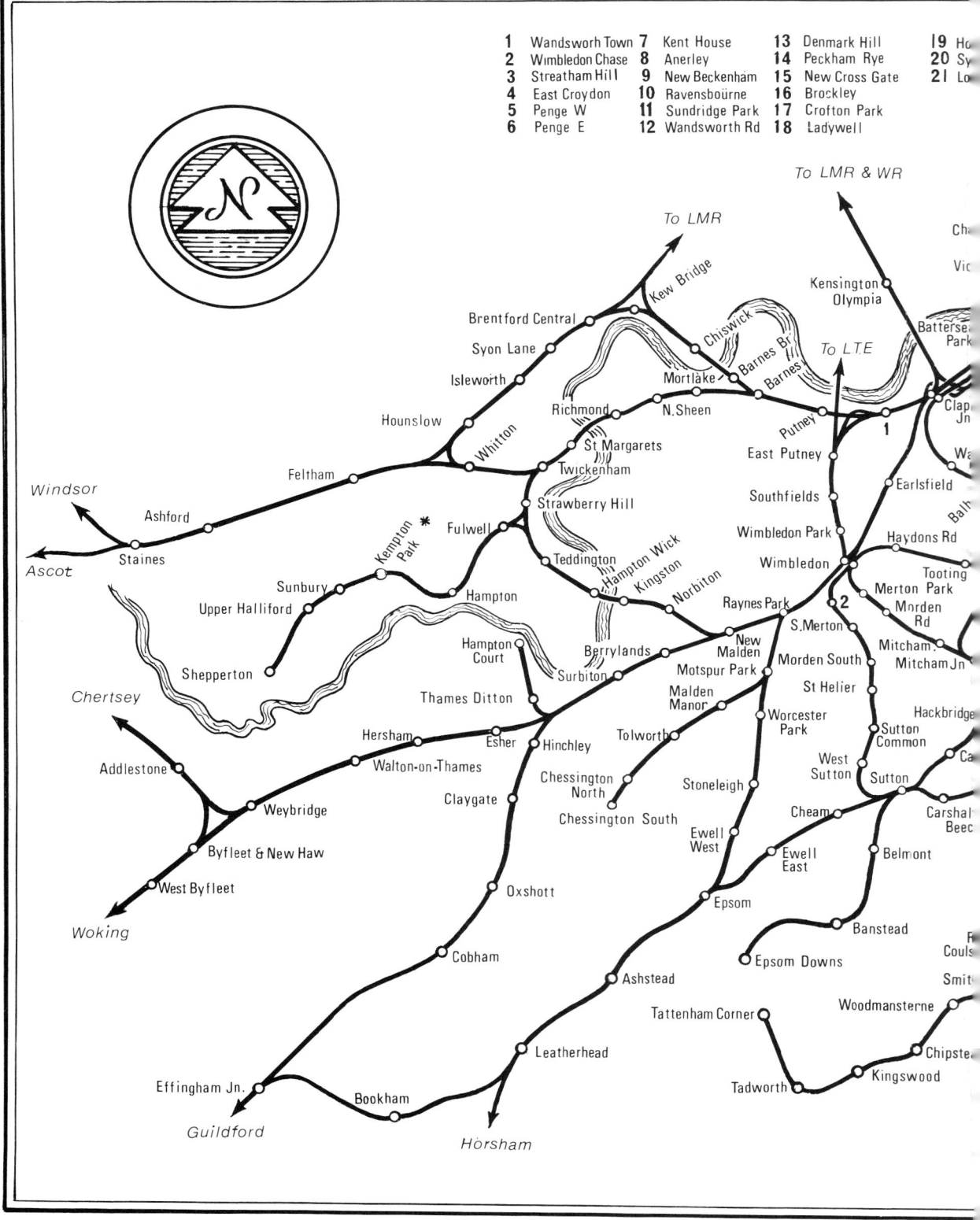

1	Wandsworh Town	7	Kent House	13	Denmark Hill	19	Ho
2	Wimbledon Chase	8	Anerley	14	Peckham Rye	20	Sy
3	Streatham Hill	9	New Beckenham	15	New Cross Gate	21	Lo
4	East Croydon	10	Ravensbourne	16	Brockley		
5	Penge W	11	Sundridge Park	17	Crofton Park		
6	Penge E	12	Wandsworth Rd	18	Ladywell		